D1239970

The Parent's Guide to College for Students on the Autism Spectrum

The Parent's Guide to College for Students on the Autism Spectrum

Jane Thierfeld Brown, EdD,
Lorraine E. Wolf, PhD,
Lisa King, MEd,
and G. Ruth Kukiela Bork, MEd

P.O. Box 23173
Shawnee Mission, Kansas 66283-0173
www.aapcpublishing.net

© 2012 AAPC Publishing
P.O. Box 23173
Shawnee Mission, Kansas 66283-0173
www.aapcpublishing.net • 913.897.1004

Publisher's Cataloging-in-Publication

The parent's guide to college for students on the autism spectrum /
Jane Thierfeld Brown ... [et al.] -- Shawnee Mission, Kan. : AAPC Pub.,
c2012.

    p. ; cm.

    ISBN: 978-1-934575-89-5
    LCCN: 2011943592
    Companion title to: Students with Asperger syndrome: a guide
    for college personnel.
    Includes bibliographical references.

    1. Autism spectrum disorders--Patients--Education (Higher)
2. Autistic people--Education (Higher) 3. Asperger's syndrome--
Patients--Education (Higher) 4. Parents of autistic children--
Handbooks, manuals, etc. I. Brown, Jane Thierfeld. II. Students
with Asperger syndrome: a guide for college personnel.

LC4717.5 .P37 2012
371.94--dc23   1112

This book is designed in Boton and Times New Roman.

Printed in the United States of America.

Acknowledgments

Our sincere thanks to the hundreds of parents who have shared their children, their stories, and their challenges with us.

Our sincere thanks to all of the students we have worked with over the years. You have taught us and guided us in ways we never even imagined.

Our sincere thanks to all the educators who return day after day to help their students move onward and upward.

Our sincere thanks to the clinicians who work with all our children on the autism spectrum.

And, finally, to our families, you are the inspiration for our work, the spark for our passion, and the love that fuels our motivation. Thank you all.

Jane Thierfeld Brown
Lorraine Wolf
Lisa King
Ruth Bork

Table of Contents

Introduction

College students on the autism spectrum are becoming increasingly common on U.S. campuses. In the late 1990s when the authors presented at a national conference of disability services providers, most of the attendees had never heard of Asperger Syndrome or other autism spectrum disorders. And those who did have experience with this population were mystified and concerned about how to best provide services, support success, and deal with the problems that inevitably arose during the college experience. The interest in our presentation was dramatic, with overflow seating on a Saturday afternoon. Yet, no one in attendance could have predicted the increase in numbers they were to see over the next decade. And none of us could have predicted that so many colleges and universities today not only know about autism spectrum disorders but are proactive in designing programs to support students.

Yet, despite such progress, school districts, families, educators, and health professionals across the country struggle daily with planning for life after high school, deciding whether college is appropriate, and if so, what kind of college, how far from home, and what kinds of services their student will need. No two students with autism spectrum disorders are alike. Each requires individual planning, goals, and resources to succeed. There is no one-size fits all. No college is appropriate for all students with autism spectrum disorders, and no student is a good fit for every college. The goodness-of-fit achieved and the planning that goes into the transition to college is often the single best predictor of student success. It is with this in mind that we bring our collective expertise and experience as university disability service providers, clinicians, educators, and parents to writing this book.*

For ease of reading, throughout this book, instead of referring to students as "on the autism spectrum" or "with Asperger Syndrome," we will refer to them simply as students with AS.

We are disability services providers with over 100 years of combined experience. Some of us are also parents of kids on the autism spectrum. We all know how families feel from diagnosis to adulthood, from good years in school with great practitioners to difficult years. We have all faced, or are facing, transitions after school, transitions away from entitlement laws (see below). We have learned that regardless of the amount of planning and expert help, there will be tough times. However, we know that knowledge, awareness, and preparation assist with navigating rough seas ahead.

This volume concentrates on providing families, clinicians, teachers, and high school specialists information about the transition to college. We are aware that higher education is not appropriate for all students on the autism spectrum and that job training is an equal or better postsecondary option for some families (including one of the authors' children). However, many students with AS benefit greatly from college, and we believe that students who can benefit from higher education should have that opportunity.

As parents, teachers, and clinicians, our commitment is to help ensure that students with AS become successful. As with more typical students, we hope they earn good grades, are comfortable in the classroom, and enjoy extracurricular activities, clubs, sports – all that college life entails. As we write this book, we realize that good intentions do not always lead to independence and success in adulthood. The success many students experience in high school is, in part, due to a carefully planned curriculum, complete with a team of supports – not the least of which is the parent. However, this level of support is rarely available on most college campuses. In order to succeed in college, students must be able to navigate a complex social world and academic rigor simultaneously. For some students on the spectrum this is attainable; others require assistance.

It has been said that parents interpret their child with AS to the world and interpret the world to their child. Once a child is launched from home into college, who will act as the interpreter? Over the last decade, we have seen postsecondary programs being developed all over the world. All such programs struggle to develop means to interpret college to students. Programs continue to expand each year. We do not list individual programs in this book, as that information would be outdated before the book is even published. Rather, we list some programs on our website, www.CollegeAutismSpectrum.com. Each family must investigate, call, visit, and investigate again prior to selecting an individual postsecondary option.

Many students with AS benefit greatly from college, and we believe that students who can benefit from higher education should have that opportunity.

This is an exciting time for people with AS. Services and programs are constantly evolving, yet in many areas of the country, services only exist up to age 18. As with all of our children, those with AS spend up to four times as long as adults as they do as kids, and as a society, we must provide preparation for adulthood for students with AS. The alternative is to leave growing numbers of our population to a life of needing care rather than being able to care for themselves and living satisfying adult lives, making useful contributions to society. As postsecondary educators, we believe that college may provide the best launching pad for students who are able to use it.

As you read this book, we ask that you keep an open mind about your student and what he or she may or may not accomplish. Not everyone must graduate from college, and some students who do graduate from college are not successful adults. Some students need one or two years after high school before starting college; others need to go part time while working and practicing life skills. There is no *one* way to be successful, no matter how many friends and neighbors believe there may be. Sometimes

Each family must investigate, call, visit, and investigate again prior to selecting an individual postsecondary option.

our students are more successful than we anticipate, so keep your mind open to that possibility as well. More than anything, be realistic about your hopes and dreams and ask the student to do the same. Is your student holding himself back or are you? Is the student being realistic enough or does she need a trusted adult to explain things? An open mind will make this book most useful to you and to your student.

Significant changes to diagnostic practice and standard nomenclature are in the works that will have a large impact on how we refer to a range of diagnoses currently falling under the "autism" umbrella. These changes will affect familiar terminology such that diagnostic distinctions between types of pervasive developmental disorders will no longer be made, while some diagnostic labels may vanish altogether. With this change, the diagnostic term of choice will change to "autism spectrum disorders."

Philosophically, we believe in the continuum of the autism spectrum, regardless of the specific diagnosis assigned. We believe that postsecondary options similarly are tailored to the individual, not to the diagnosis. For that reason, we feel that interventions designed for students with "Asperger Syndrome" could be just as effective for students with high-functioning autism, pervasive developmental disorders-not otherwise specified (PDD-NOS), or nonverbal learning disabilities (NVLD). In keeping with this philosophy, we will refer to "students with AS" or "students on the spectrum" throughout the book.

More than anything, be realistic about your hopes and dreams and ask the student to do the same.

In addition, while the prevalence of AS is greater in males than in females, we will alternate pronouns through the book in recognition of the many girls and young women with AS we have encountered. We are optimistic that whichever direction diagnostic processes take, students can and will thrive in college to the extent that families, students, educators, and college administrators are aware and open to change.

What You Can Expect

This book is arranged in the order your family will go through the college process from looking at where you have been and where your student is going, to how to look for a college, the admissions process, etc. Each chapter begins with an overview and a vignette of a student and where he or she is in the college process. The vignettes are about different students to make the examples as comprehensive as possible in hopes that readers will find issues from their own family in some of them.

.

CHAPTER 1

Where Have You Been and Where Are You Going?

*Luke's family never thought they would get this far.
Luke got in! The tears and the battles with the school
district have all paid off. Luke's father has called the college
and demanded a meeting with disability services.*

*The parents (without Luke) arrive for the meeting armed
with the transition plan and the testing results from ninth
grade, which support eligibility for special education.
Luke's dad states that Luke requires the services of an aide
in class, oral exams in lieu of papers, unlimited time for
tests in a separate location (preferably open-book, open-
notebook, take-home), and not to have to take English or
math. He concludes by saying that if their son does not get
these supports, they will bring in their advocate, and maybe their lawyer. The Disability Services provider refuses to
hold the meeting without Luke. Maybe Luke and his family
are not as prepared as they thought ...*

In this chapter, we will review the steps that families have
typically taken en route to getting their children educated
and eventually sending a youngster with AS to college. To
have gotten to this point, families have been tenacious in
getting a good education for their student. We believe that
if all understand the process of what comes before and what
will come after, the transition to college will be smoother.

Families of typical children celebrate graduation with a mix of pride and eager anticipation for the departure of their offspring. Of course, there are doubts, fights, and struggles along the way, but for the most part things have worked out pretty much as planned. Families of children with AS travel a very different path, one that is often marked by confusion, bewildering questions, and few resources.

Most parents of teens with disabilities will tell you that it is difficult to navigate the special education and medical minefields successfully enough to be at the college transition point. We believe that the cornerstone of successful transition for teens with AS is a good partnership between the family and the college of choice, the student, and the family. To best foster this relationship, it is vitally important that everyone understand the transition process from the family's point of view.

Where Are Families Coming From?

Receiving a diagnosis of AS is a complicated and painful process, often dating back to the child's infancy. Prior to being diagnosed with AS, most children have been evaluated by teams of doctors, therapists, and other professionals and have collected multiple diagnoses. As part of the process to find an answer to their children's difficulties, parents may have investigated countless treatments, fought with their insurance companies, and battled with school districts.

Having secured a diagnosis, parents must deal with the devastation that comes with a diagnosis of an autistic disorder and all that it implies. For most, this involves grieving over the perfect child they dreamed of and adjusting their expectations to accept the child they have. Educational, caretaking, employment, and other financial circumstances will change drastically as the family comes to terms with the impact of having a child diagnosed with a severe developmental disorder. Families and caregivers enter a confusing maze of interventions and options as they learn how to secure services for their child.

This often painful process may last for years, with some families never reaching the stage of full acceptance of the AS diagnosis. Some families bring their sense of anger and disappointment to the college transition process and enter this stage ready to take on another battle for their child.

Receiving a diagnosis of AS is a complicated and painful process, often dating back to the child's infancy.

However, battling college personnel is not a fruitful way to start the transition, and parents need to understand that there are legal as well as philosophical reasons for having to shift their perspective from a parent-owned-and-operated corporation to one run by the student. Nevertheless, the transition process is achieved by the family as a whole, and there are many instances in which parental involvement is valuable.

In order to look at where your child is going, we must first look at where he or she, and you, have been as a family. One of the more difficult aspects of raising a child on the spectrum is securing appropriate education services.

Special Education and the Law

One of the core challenges for families raising a child with AS is learning to secure appropriate educational services. Educational and remedial services (there may be many, including speech-language therapy, occupational therapy, and counseling) may be provided to eligible students with AS. Because of the high cost of securing such services privately, as well as the logistical demands of transporting the child to and from a multitude of appointments, it has been essential that parents become skilled in the art of negotiating these services through their school system. However, parents learn quickly that constant monitoring of mandated service delivery (in and out of school) is often necessary to advocate for their child and to achieve the best outcome. These skills are hard won, and we understand it is difficult to change. At the cost of repetition, we will review special education law as a means to understand the differences that will be faced in college.

Differences in the Laws	
Individuals With Disabilities Education Act (IDEA)	**Americans With Disabilities Act (ADA)**
Responsibility on parent/ school for provision of services	Responsibility on the student to initiate provision of services
Ensures success	Ensures equal access
IDEA: Education law	ADA: Civil rights law
Entitlement	Eligibility
Special accommodations	Reasonable accommodations
Focus on diagnostic label	Focus on functional impact
Disability = One of 13 categories	Disability = Impairment + Substantial Limitation + Major Life Activity

The Individuals With Disabilities Education Act (IDEA) (http://idea.ed.gov) is the education act that guarantees special education and related services to eligible children with disabilities in public schools grades K-12 (and special early intervention for at risk or diagnosed preschool children and toddlers). IDEA provides federal money to state and local school districts to cover (some) of the costs of educating students with disabilities.

IDEA (and its recent reauthorization IDEIA or Individuals With Disabilities Education Improvement Act) mandates that educational systems provide an individualized program designed to meet specific educational needs, including a free and appropriate education in the least restrictive environment. School districts are thus required to identify and assess at-risk children or may do so at the request of a parent or teacher. This assessment is a multidisciplinary evaluation with various members of the special education and teaching staff, and may include comprehensive educational, cognitive, personality, speech, language, occupational, and physical therapy assessments. This process may (or may not) culminate in a diagnostic formulation. Under IDEA, students become eligible for special education and related services by being diagnosed with one of several medical or psychological conditions. A child with an autism spectrum diagnosis of any type is usually eligible, although services are not always guaranteed. Also, it is important to understand that the criteria that govern diagnosis and service vary widely between districts and between states.

IDEA (and its recent reauthorization) mandates that educational systems provide an individualized program designed to meet specific educational needs, including a free and appropriate education in the least restrictive environment.

Individualized Education Program (IEP)

Once a student has been diagnosed and qualifies, the interdisciplinary team develops an IEP that details the services and accommodations the child is to receive (including what, when, who, and how). The law dictates the time period within which this plan must be developed. The IEP is ratified in an interdisciplinary meeting with the parents, the (older) student, and an advocate, if they so choose. Further, IDEA requires periodic reassessment and reframing of goals to determine if the student still qualifies for services and if changes to the plan are warranted. Parents must participate in the IEP process and have the right to approve or reject the plan.

They may call for a re-review of the student and the plans at any time (see Disability Rights and Education Defense Fund, http://www. dredf.org, for more information; also see http://www.wrightslaw. com).

Families and professionals must understand that the transition plan does not require students to be retested.

Most important in this context:
IDEA coverage lasts only until high school graduation or age 21, whichever comes first (this may vary in some states and for some conditions). The IEP language requires that high schools engage the student and the family in transition planning for all graduating seniors. Families and professionals must understand that the transition plan does not require students to be retested. This is often a source of confusion when students are asked for current documentation of disability when they arrive at college.

The 504 Plan

Some students only need accommodation such as extra time for exams. Usually such students would not qualify for the full range of special education services guaranteed under the IEP discussed above.

A 504 Plan may be developed when (a) a student has a disability not ordinarily covered by special education (e.g., attention deficit disorder), or (b) the student only requires minimal assistance such as exam accommodations alone. Thus, 504 Plans are used by many school districts as a means to grant accommodations such as extra time or permission to use computers on exams without providing any special remedial or therapeutic interventions to students who are not otherwise eligible for special education services. This category often includes students with milder AS as "other health impaired" students.

Because the name "504 Plan" derives from Section 504 of the Rehabilitation Act, which governs services in college (see Chapter 5 for more details), parents and guidance counselors often mistakenly believe that this plan carries over to college, and assume the related documentation is automatically acceptable to colleges and universities. This is not the case. Unfortunately, families then miss the opportunity to have their son or daughter re-evaluated while still covered under IDEA and must seek private, expensive testing. Please discuss testing with your student's high school while there is time to do a new evaluation to be used in college. It is up to you to work with your district and to call individual colleges to determine their policies.

> *Eric has been on campus for four weeks. He has been making it to his classes and doing his homework (although he has not handed in the labs for his chemistry class). He failed a test for which he did not receive any accommodations. Before classes began, Eric's mother had called the disability office to discuss Eric's situation and was told to send documentation and have Eric make an appointment. She sent the IEP as well as a prescription pad with a scrawled diagnosis of "PDD-NOS" from the neurologist who diagnosed Eric when he was 8 years old. She included a note instructing disability staff that Eric will require extra time, papers and essays to be handwritten in pencil, no penalty for spelling errors, shorter reading assignments, and waiver of the college math requirement. Since these accommodations were provided in high school under his 504 Plan, she was confident he would automatically receive them in college as well.*
>
> *When Eric tells his parents he failed a test, his mom asks him about the accommodations. He remembers that Disability Services had sent him a letter a few weeks ago telling him*

*that his documentation of disability was incomplete and in-
structing him to make an appointment to discuss the request
that had been made on his behalf. His parents are furious
that Disability Services did not properly accommodate his
disability and have called the dean.*

Where Are Families Going?

As part of the transition, families will confront (or be confronted
with) a seismic shift in the legal protections their student may enjoy. Recall that IDEA previously covered access to special education and related services (including in many cases accommodations,
evaluation and assessment, adjunctive services such as clinical services, aides, and/or transportation). When your son or daughter becomes an adult, however, he or she moves from the familiar world
of IDEA to the world of the Americans With Disabilities Act (and
its 2009 revision, the Americans with Disabilities Amendment Act
(ADA; http://www.ada.gov) and Section 504 of the Rehabilitation
Act (http://www.dol.gov/oasam/regs/statutes/sec504.htm). We will
discuss the new legal framework in detail in Chapter 5.

In our experience, the source of many conflicts families experience
with their colleges of choice is unfamiliarity (coupled with shock
and surprise) with the way colleges view students legally. You have
become expert advocates, well accustomed to swinging statutes and
threats to make the educational system work for your child. College is
going to be very different, but no one tells you that.

Your student has left the world of entitlement to education, and is
preparing to enter the world of access to an educational program.
Very different meanings here. Entitlement guaranteed your child's
rights to an education. Access provides your adult student protection from discrimination. Period. It can be difficult to adjust to this
change. The mandates under which colleges operate and the tools

needed to navigate have shifted under your feet. In Chapter 5 you will learn about civil rights and higher education. For now, understand that the changes which will support your student's development into an independent and successful adult start with accepting that nothing will be familiar.

Families find that the roles change for everyone as the student goes off to college. Parents may have great difficulty separating from their child with AS in more ways than just the physical move away from home. You must now learn to trust that your student has sound judgment and will understand what to do in a new and different environment. Parents have learned to act as the main advocate and CEO for their child's education to this point. Families who anticipate this change and begin the process as early as middle school often find that the shift in responsibility is smoother.

We believe that students should enter college with the following sets of competencies already in place.

Critical Student Attributes
- Is prepared for life after high school
- Demonstrates appropriate study habits and other academic skills
- Is organized, timely, and neat
- Knows and displays proper classroom etiquette
- Has effective social skills
- Interacts with different people across settings
- Deals with criticism, feedback, or rejection
- Resists peer pressure (drugs, drinking, dating)
- Structures environment
- Knows how to use leisure time
- Knows and articulates needs (incl. medical)
- Masters basic adaptive daily living skills (transportation, cooking, laundry, etc.)

Shift in Responsibility		
Issues	**Secondary**	**Postsecondary**
Identification	School/Parent/Team	Student
Assessment	School/Team	Student
Programming	School/Parent/Team	Student & Institution
Advocacy	School/Parent/Team	Student/OSD
Decision Making	IEP Team	Student
Transition Planning	IEP Team	Student
Arranging Accommodations	Team and Teachers	Student

Relinquishing the role of CEO and teaching their son or daughter with AS to manage her or his life and education is scary for most families. Students and their parents must understand that the college student now has certain legal rights and responsibilities. The student must become his or her own CEO and self-advocate. The student must take on this role in the new legal framework in which he will operate, since the college or university considers students over age 18 to be adults. For example, for what might be the first time in their young lives, students now can invoke their rights to privacy, which extends beyond "don't come into my room" and can totally exclude parental involvement. They are now also held accountable for complying with a host of policies, procedures, and codes of conduct (academic and behavioral) that will govern many aspects of their lives in college.

In the following, we present a model transition plan, which outlines the ideal scenario. Don't worry if yours has not followed this sequence. It is not too late to change or repair things.

Comprehensive Timeline From H.S. to College Entrance

9th and 10th grade
1. Attendance and participation in IEP meetings in which the student articulates his disability, strengths, and needs
2. Creation and use of time management system for class assignments and out of class activities
3. Classroom accommodations to be negotiated directly with teachers rather than pull-outs to resource room
4. Increasing independence at home, making student responsible for managing and being accountable for free time and academic demands

11th and 12th grade
1. Work with guidance counselor to develop list of possible colleges. Begin to research online and visit
2. Finalize Transition IEP. Student should increase participation and initiation of all things related to their services
3. Participate in summer jobs or volunteer activities
4. Practice interviewing skills
5. Apply to college

Admissions Process
1. Family meets with school counselor to draw up list of schools that might be appropriate given the student's grades, class ranking, test scores (SAT or ACT), interests
2. Families visit campuses, look online to refine the choice
3. Application materials arrives, complete forms, requests for letters of recommendation, transcripts, and a form for the personal essay
4. Complete application materials and submit by the deadline!

Interviewing
1. Consult the college counselor about the typical college interview and coach the student
2. Role play and rehearse in preparation for the interview
3. Prepare the script or narrative in advance of the interview – and stick to it as much as possible
4. Consider disclosing if there any unusual speech or interaction features that would stand out to the interviewer.
5. Dress neatly and comfortably. Do not dress in attire that would be a distraction for the student
6. Practice handshakes and eye contact
7. Reduce anxiety by arriving early or checking out the environment in advance
8. Inquire about alternate arrangements to a group interview (if one is required) if this type of interview is not suitable to the student's abilities

Comprehensive Timeline From H.S. to College Entrance

After Receiving Acceptance Letter
1. Follow procedure outlined in the letter for confirming acceptance and sending in deposit to hold spot
2. Contact Disability Services to formally register with them for accommodations during school year
3. Inquire about Open House through Disability Services
4. Inquire about any assistance needed during summer orientation (i.e., dorm accommodations, activities student must participate in)

After Attending Orientation
1. Create New Student Resource List with relevant support providers, on-and-off-campus co-curricular resources (i.e., barber, ATMs, restaurants, etc.)
2. Contact Disability Services for possible housing accommodations, Disability Services Open House
3. Visit campus to walk schedule, visit pertinent offices
4. Get familiar with school email, online course management system, etc.
5. Consider meeting with Disability Services in late August to set up schedule, create pre-semester checklist of prof. contacts, purchasing books, etc.

Final Month Prior to Arrival on Campus
1. Make sure meds are current, working, and refill plan is identified
2. Get into good sleep/wake cycle. Buy and use alarm clock
3. Practice all daily living skills independently
4. Practice using a time management schedule if not already
5. Contact Res Life for look at room arrangement if possible
6. Contact new roommate if appropriate and establish basic preferences for living together. Can seek help from Res Life or Disability Services if needed
7. Use Stress Management Scale to identify triggers and strategies
8. Shop for room and study essentials
9. Meet with Disability Services to consider early contact with instructors, obtaining early syllabus and purchasing books

Welcome to College!

Many students and their parents are not prepared for the many ways in which college is different from high school. Reviewing the differences, talking to current and recent college students, and talking to personnel at (any) college will help you understand some of the key differences. We will highlight some of these differences below and in the table "Differences Between High School and College" on page 22.

1. *Cognitive and academic demands get more sophisticated.*
    Beginning college students (with or without disabilities) need more advanced skills to cope with the greater academic and cognitive demands of college. Few students arrive at college fully appreciating that the skills they developed in high school are likely not up to the task. Many find they need additional instruction in how to prepare for and behave in the classroom. ·Successful students eventually learn to advocate for themselves with their teachers, with administrators, and with staff to survive and succeed. They will need new and better study habits and learn to take more and different types of larger and harder tests (essay, multiple choice, short answer, etc.).

    Students must figure out what to do and what not to do as they prepare for class. They may not realize that their professors are entitled to deduct points for lateness and missed deadlines and that there will not be any reminders on the board or at the beginning of class of when a project is due. Students with AS, in particular, need to comprehend the hierarchy and the rules of the classroom as they relate to staying seated, not interrupting, raising one's hand, etc.

2. *College professors expect students to be sophisticated thinkers* and have good reasoning abilities. They can and do expect that students possess good abstract abilities, including categorical thinking and use of logic and sequence. Students need to be able to make inferences and draw conclusions by integrating and synthesizing information from multiple sources to perform at the college level. Their writing must be logical, per-

suasive, and grammatically correct. Spelling errors may result in lost points, even in a paper for a science class. Students are expected to think for themselves and to construct and develop their own new ideas.

3. *Time management.* College freshmen, in general, are unprepared for some of the changes that they find when they come to college. Many look forward with great anticipation to the freedom that they will have once they leave home and are on their own.

Without the familiar helping hand of their parents and the guidance and support of their high school teachers, this "freedom" leaves many students adrift during their first term at college.

But often their thoughts about freedom are focused on how they plan to use their social time, without much thought being given to the freedom that they will have in planning their academic time and responsibilities. Thus, they are often unprepared to make the adjustments necessary to function successfully in an environment that provides them total freedom in the academic area. With only 12 to 16 hours per week of classroom time and no formal scheduled sports or music activities, medical appointments, or curfews, students may find themselves with many hours per day of unscheduled time. Yet, they are unlikely to have had prior experience in managing this time, which has always been planned and monitored by teachers and parents. Without the familiar helping hand of their parents and the guidance and support of their high school teachers, this "freedom" leaves many students adrift during their first term at college. Often students on the spectrum feel even more lost with these "extra" hours. Without guidance, many find themselves using their time in an unproductive fashion or sleeping at irregular hours, with the result that their sleep-wake cycle can get turned around so that they sleep through daytime (especially morning) classes and meals.

4. *Exams take on more importance.* Another area where new students are typically under- or unprepared is the college exam structure. For the first time, courses may have a mid-term and a final exam, or even only a final exam. Most high school students are unfamiliar with this model and have not been schooled in how to plan and study for courses where the grade is based on a few cumulative exams. Students on the spectrum may be thrown into confusion, chaos, or even panic when faced with the need to study for courses structured in this fashion.

5. *The role of college professors is very different.* Another difference between high school and college is the degree of involvement teachers have in students' out-of-class preparation and classroom attendance. College faculty may or may not take attendance, but many state attendance policies for their class and deduct grades for unexcused absences. An illness that results in being absent for several days or a single absence because of weather-related flight delays could catapult a student into a grade reduction. A socially skilled student might be able to present his or her case in negotiating a resolution; however, few students with AS understand how this must be done. Further, it is not unusual for students with AS to miss class out of fear or confusion about how to handle incomplete homework assignments. Unable to troubleshoot, these students may simply conclude they cannot attend the class.

For some students, an inability to figure out the proper course of action given the fact that they missed a deadline can begin the slippery slope to missing many classes. Parents sometimes admit that their student can do all of the work but does not remember to hand in her homework or term paper. Such statements are often couched in a request that someone be assigned to check that the student hands in his work, but parents do need to understand that a homework helper/checker is not a service that is usually available. College faculty frequently do not monitor students' completion of homework assign-

For some students, an inability to figure out the proper course of action given the fact that they missed a deadline can begin the slippery slope to missing many classes.

ments until a considerable amount of time has elapsed. By then, students may face a grade reduction or the obligation to make up missed assignments before the end of the term. The additional challenge for students in the more technical fields is that lecture material and associated homework comprise the building blocks upon which the next level of classroom lecture and homework are built. In such courses, therefore, several missed homework assignments could throw a student into a situation where he can no longer follow along in the course.

Differences Between High School and College		
Item	High School	College
Residence Life	• Student has own room/bathroom • Has privacy, personal space • Can keep room any way he/she likes	• Student may have to share a bathroom • Has to shower with others • Involves participating in communal living • May have roommates with different schedules, different styles

Differences Between High School and College		
Item	**High School**	**College**
Dining	• Student can eat what, where, and when he or she wishes • Parents supply food in the house	• Dining hall may not have student's particular likes • Student may have to eat with others • Food available only at prescribed times
Routines	• Student may have same classes every day • Classes are held in same place • Transportation is provided by parents	• Class schedule or place of meeting may change at the last minute • Each day's schedule is different from the next • Student may have to use public transportation or walk
Instruction	Teachers may … • Check student's notes for accuracy • Interpret or modify assignments • Remind student of deadlines • Allow time for homework, research, and study during class • Tell student what to study for the tests	• Student is responsible for checking syllabus, asking for help from professors, and seeking tutors • Teachers rarely teach directly from the textbook. They challenge students to think analytically and to synthesize information • Student must synthesize info from text, notes, lectures, and other sources for tests • Class time only allows for instruction (50-min. classes). All research, study, and homework must be done on student's own time

Differences Between High School and College		
Item	**High School**	**College**
Time Manage-ment	• Parents and teachers help student follow schedules, break down projects into smaller units • Structure is built into the school day • Limits are set by others (parents, school)	• Student makes choices between studying versus lots of other temptations • Student must judge and plan for time needed to complete assignments • Student must juggle many competing priorities • Student must manage own leisure time
Studying	• Studying is usually synonymous with doing homework • Student may not have to study to make A's • Class time is set aside for study	• Student must rewrite lecture notes, paraphrase information from reading assignments, summarize and integrate information from a variety of sources (e.g., texts, class lectures and library assignments) • Higher level thinking is required; more than memorization
Disability Issues	• Teachers figure out what student needs in order to be successful and inform others • Parents and teachers know student's needs, strengths, and weaknesses • Teachers modify student's classes and curriculum • Teachers make waivers for difficult subjects • School must do whatever it takes to help the student succeed	• Student must initiate • Student must disclose the nature of disability to obtain accommodations • College gets to determine reasonableness • College may not waiver requirements or make substitutions • Student must be otherwise qualified (academically, behaviorally)

Differences Between High School and College		
Item	**High School**	**College**
Class Size	• Student might receive one-to-one help • Sometimes there are 10-20 students in class	• Student must seek help from professor • There may be 500 students in each class
Tests	• Usually take place after each chapter • Quizzes are often given weekly • Tests are usually multiple choice or true/false	• Could be two midterms and a final • Essay questions require synthesizing information • Spelling, grammar, sentence structure, etc., are graded as well as content
Assign-ments	• Teachers assign day to day • Student can write the paper the night before • Student may choose preferred assignments or projects	• The student is expected to follow the semester syllabus • It is the student's responsibility to plan ahead • Student must learn how to break large assignment into smaller units to be completed over the course of the semester
Behavior	• Inappropriate behavior is often accepted as part of disability ("manifest determination")*	• Must be able to abide by the conduct code, treat others in respectful, non-abusive manner
Stress	• Student can go to teacher's room to de-stress whenever needed • Someone provides student with missed information, as needed	• Student may have to locate safe place in proximity to each class; still expected to have all notes and materials • Student has to manage novel and stress-producing situations daily

* *"A process whereby the behavior of a student who receives special education is considered to determine if the actions that resulted in the consideration of some disciplinary action against the student were manifestations of the student's dsability" (http://definitions.uselegal. com/m/manifestation-determination/).*

In this chapter we reviewed some of the changes your student will encounter when moving from the more protected environment of high school to college, including some important things to look for when researching potential schools. The prospect of college for a student on the spectrum can be one of anxiety and doubt for the entire family, and there are very few guideposts on how to get there. In the next chapter, we will introduce you to the process of searching for the right fit in a college.

Miles desperately wants to attend college because he has found the work in high school not to be challenging enough. He thinks that in college he will finally be able to take advanced math classes to his heart's content. He has used a full-time aide in high school, which was tapered off in 11th grade. His strategy tutor and resource room teacher have been working with him on learning how to plan and organize his time. He now (well, most of the time) uses his smart phone to enter assignments and appointments, and he knows how to back it up and print out his schedule each evening. There are white boards in almost every room of the house with reminders of things to do. The next step for him is to try to use the local mass transit, but he has been too scared to go by himself.

CHAPTER 2

Finding the Right College

Andrew is an 18-year-old high school senior. Although legally an adult, he has never been away from home. Unlike his younger sister, he never went to camp, sleepovers were rare, and he is most comfortable in the familiarity of his bedroom at home. His videogames, his computer, and his childhood Lego sets are his prized possessions. He has never been a joiner and has never liked sports, but he has always been a good student. His guidance counselor has told his family that he must consider a four-year competitive university since his grade point average is A-, his SAT scores are above the 95th percentile, and his class rank is in the top 10. Andrew has always been interested in musical theater and has participated in a few community productions. He is also passionate about climate change, weather patterns, and globalization. He collects sports statistics, especially football. He has no idea of possible career goals. His parents want him to complete college and earn a professional degree so that he may be self-supported.

Excited by the prospect of college, the family is ready to start their search. Andrew is thinking about the state he wants to live in. The family has consulted a college placement advisor who is less sure that students with AS should attend college or that they can succeed. As a result, she has encouraged the family to consider vocational options. Andrew has never had a job but has always been a student, and the family decides to embark on a college search. Although they agree their son should consider college, especially Andrew's father who envisions fraternity life and games for his son, his mother is not sure Andrew is ready to move away. After months of considering the options, the family has narrowed it down to a few choices. Choice number one would be community college close to home where Andrew could live at home. Option two (Andrew's favorite) is the large state university three hours from home with 60,000 students. Andrew has seen the football team on television and likes the colors. Choice number three is a small progressive college in another state. This college has no grades or core requirements. All students are required to live in small multi-student apartments.

How are they going to make these decisions?

In this chapter we discuss the choice of college. We will outline many of the features students and families must consider when deciding whether college is the best current option. If the answer to pursuing college is a resounding "yes," we outline some steps to help families select among the hundreds (maybe thousands) of colleges out there and how to evaluate whether a particular college is appropriate for an individual student. Various college environments are considered, as well as selected facets of the admission and application process, including the college essay and interview and disclosure of a student's AS.

A s the opening vignette demonstrates, many factors are involved in searching for, deciding on, and applying to a postsecondary option. Andrew and his family are embarking on a typical scenario for a not-so-typical young man. While Andrew's academic choice is not constrained by poor grades, class rank, or test scores, his ability to attend and thrive in college is less clear. Like most 18-year-olds, he has no idea of what he wants to do when he grows up. Academically, he probably could major in anything and do well; however, his family is aware that the residential and extracurricular aspects of going away to school will pose challenges.

So many decisions, so many choices! Living at home in familiar surroundings? Would that be academically challenging enough? Could he ever learn to drive and be trusted with a car? Would he be able to live away from home and have a roommate? Could he stand someone sharing his space? Could he manage to travel home during holidays and breaks? Structure or no structure? Requirements or no requirements?

All families sending children to college face these choices and questions. But when the child is a student with AS, decisions must be made that are much more specific to the individual needs of that youngster. Nothing that has occurred in elementary, middle, or high school comes close to this choice. In this chapter, we will explore some of the factors illustrated in the vignette above.

The Search Process

Every family considering college for a son or daughter should conduct a thorough search to find the right college. For students with AS, it is even more important to search carefully before making a choice. Successful transition to college depends on a good fit between the student and the campus. When an inflexible student meets a rigid campus, the chances of a successful outcome are less than one might hope. For example, a student who only wants to study Japanese animé and attends a small liberal arts college may find it necessary to take two years of general education courses and some general computer courses before being introduced to computer animation. Then the student may need to learn basic drawing before moving to a specialization like animé. Some classes may need to be taken at another school. For some students, this detour to their end goal is frustrating, and sometimes even unacceptable.

> *Successful transition to college depends on a good fit between the student and the campus.*

Optimally, the search team should include the student, his or her family, guidance counselors, educational team, and clinical team if appropriate. Planning the college search begins at the end of the second (sophomore) or beginning of the third (junior year) year of high school. Students with AS may want to begin this process even earlier if they have exceptional trouble adapting to change. In this case, more than one visit to the same college may also be necessary.

Several planning meetings over a period of time should take place. For example, are the student's expectations realistic? Does he have unrealistic expectations due to concrete or rigid beliefs that college must only be Ivy League? Are the parents' expectations reasonable? Do they expect their son or daughter to be a legacy? Or do they underestimate their offspring's ability to move away from home? Has the clinical team's input been sought with regard to symptoms of depression and possible need for ongoing intervention? Have IEP goals and documentation been updated with the educational team? Will accommodations for entrance exams be sought? All members of the team have important input, and everyone's voice is important.

In the following, we will discuss some key points for the college search, ranked in importance as:
1. Residential or commuter campus
2. Distance from home
3. Size
4. Curriculum of interest
5. Specialized program or disability service

Families are encouraged to use the following checklist as a means to illuminate and articulate preferences and concerns regarding the differences between types of higher education settings. We suggest that parents and their student fill out a form separately, checking off what they perceive as the relevant pros and cons to each variable. After completing the checklist, families can discuss reasons for their choices with each other or with a member of the student's support team in order to help target or prioritize the most critical categories for the particular student.

College Comparison	
Pros	**Cons**
Commuter	
☐ Added supervision/support ☐ Less financial risk ☐ Foundation courses less demanding ☐ Work on independent living skills at home ☐ Support network in place (therapist, counselors) ☐ Fewer new variables to manage ☐ Predictability	☐ Less campus community ☐ Less challenge/motivation ☐ Transportation needed ☐ Harder to join clubs or organizations ☐ May not offer student's program of interest
Residential	
☐ Opportunity for role models ☐ Participate in campus community ☐ Peers of similar age/interests ☐ More responsibilities	☐ More variables to manage ☐ More costly ☐ Less structure, supervision ☐ More responsibilities ☐ Shared space

College Comparison	
Pros	**Cons**
Close to Home	
☐ Predicable support during transition ☐ Support network in place (therapists, counselors) ☐ Fewer transportation issues ☐ Can build independence slowly	☐ Less independence ☐ Too much dependence on parents ☐ Less opportunity to create new network of friends
Far From Home	
☐ Independence ☐ Opportunities to develop new identity	☐ Difficult for parents to get there in emergency ☐ Less monitoring/supervision
Large School	
☐ Anonymity ☐ More degree options ☐ Wider variety of people (instructors) ☐ More acceptance of differences ☐ Opportunity for independence ☐ Disability Services staff more experienced ☐ Possibility of additional fee-for-service support program	☐ Anonymity ☐ Large, impersonal classes ☐ Less individual support (instructors, peers) ☐ Larger geographic area to navigate ☐ Less opportunity to meet with Disability Services
Small School	
☐ One-to-one contact ☐ Small class size ☐ More personal ☐ More contact with Disability Services	☐ Less anonymity ☐ Fewer degree choices ☐ Can have limited culture ☐ Disability Services staff may be less experienced
Urban	
☐ Wider variety of extracurricular activities ☐ Wider variety of people ☐ Mass transportation options	☐ Possible safety issues
Suburban	
☐ Limited culture ☐ Perhaps more familiar to student ☐ Less overwhelming	☐ Fewer community supports available ☐ Fewer distractions

Residential or Commuter Campus

When asked what they look forward to when going to college, most students gleefully mention the experience of living away from home and being independent. This is also one of parents' main goals for their child, a concrete sign that they have parented well. For this reason and many others, many students with AS and their parents desire this experience.

We also believe that it can be enormously important to the socially challenged young person to be living amidst a large group of peers of similar age and interest. However, the experience of living in a residence hall is destabilizing for many students with AS. Therefore, the decision to send the young person to a residential college should be a joint decision that takes into account the student's ability to cope with shared life in a residence hall far from familiar supports and routines.

> *Alice and her parents always assumed she would attend the small all-women's school her mother and aunt had attended. What they did not factor in was that all beginning students are required to live in small "houses" comprised of 3 girls per room and 15 girls per house. The girls are expected to consider the house their home and the other residents as their sisters. Alice's parents feel that this will be safe and that their daughter will make a lot of good friends, but the very idea gives Alice the creeps. More important, this is a school known for its arts programs and Alice wants to study landscape architecture of the 18th century. Due to their disagreements on this topic, Alice and her mother are not speaking at the moment. This was not a very promising start.*

Students attending residential colleges take on extra responsibilities, such as independence in their living environment (laundry, food preparation, cleaning, roommate conflicts, etc.). To cope effectively,

33

students are called on to learn effective time management and organizational strategies to bring to their personal and academic lives. Learning to manage free time and imposing structure in the absence of supervising parents and even teachers can be a daunting task. Students living away from home need to navigate an individual campus, learn to assess when they are sick or need help, and be able to learn what to do in such circumstances when Mom and Dad are far away. Often they must learn money management and budgeting skills for the first time, and most important, they must negotiate and advocate for themselves without parental involvement. Colleges and universities expect students to function as adults. Dorm mothers and bedtime check-in do not exist in typical postsecondary environments; therefore, students must be able to handle themselves independently.

In deciding whether a student is ready to live away from home, look at the large skills – Can your student make friends? What is his level of maturity? Can he comply with basic rules? Also try to envision the student engaging in many of the smaller aspects of student life. Would he independently be able to purchase textbooks at the bookstore and exchange them if he drops a course? Would he be able to use the student health services, or could he do so with simple help from family over the phone? Would he know how to call home or require assistance just to keep in touch? If the student is interested in a large campus, could he figure out how to use a bus or shuttle system to get between dormitory and classes? On smaller campuses, would she be able to find her way between buildings? Can he live with a roommate? Are there sensory sensitivities that would make group living impossible? Has he ever lived away from home before?

If the answer to any of the above questions is a resounding "no," or if the student will likely not be able to care for himself away from home, you may wish to consider a commuter campus. This provides students an opportunity to live at home and develop academic and self-care skills without the additional stresses of residential life.

Colleges and universities expect students to function as adults.

It is important that all professionals working with the family assist them as they consider whether the student is able to leave home and function independently. In our collective experience, too many students drop out of college due to residential problems because they were not prepared to fend for themselves. A well-planned transition to an environment where the student is comfortable can make all the difference.

Pros and Cons of Commuter Campuses

Commuter campuses, by definition, are close to home and include local community colleges, state colleges and universities, and even four-year Ivy League colleges, depending on where students and their family reside. The benefit of a "commuter" campus is just that. The student commutes to campus, while retaining the familiarity and comfort of home.

Yet, there are both positive and negative aspects to deciding to attend campus close to home. On the negative side, many fear that staying at home prolongs dependency. However, the student who moves away from home precipitously is often the student who returns home even more dependent and demoralized. The degree of supervision and monitoring of the student that is still possible is often a plus for families when making the decision to commute. Clinical teams, doctors, tutors, and other familiar supports remain in place, leaving the student to grapple with the academic demands of college. This may reduce stress and worry for both the student and her parents. Finally, there is less financial risk associated with sending a youngster to school while he lives at home if there are any doubts about his ability to be in residence. The time spent in college close to home or at a community college can be used as a proving ground and an opportunity to build motivation. Following this experience, a student may choose to transfer to a four-year college or move to live on campus.

The benefit of a "commuter" campus is just that. The student commutes to campus, while retaining the familiarity and comfort of home.

In many communities, there is a stigma attached to the student not leaving home after high school graduation. In some areas, smart kids are groomed for college, and nothing else is seen as valuable. In these settings, not going on to a "good college" with high bumper sticker value is seen as a failure on the part of the entire family. Interesting, this stigma often affects parents far more than the student with AS. Families have rallied for years with the goal of sending the student off to college, but sometimes families forget that getting into college is not the end of the line. Self-esteem and one's sense of worth is increased by success. Along with gains in self-esteem, when students experience success, their confidence and independence are also boosted. Conversely, these are the very attributes that can be damaged when students experience failure, such as leaving school early due to behavioral meltdowns or academic difficulties.

We do not believe that students with AS must or should be sheltered from the college experience in adolescence. However, as part of the overall planning process, it is important to consider the effect that a failed experience might have on the student and what decisions can be made that would foster success.

When young people remain at home while going to college after high school, the entire family must adapt. Parents must be comfortable establishing rules for this new adult. Siblings should understand that their brother or sister is engaged in serious schoolwork and that boundaries must be respected. If students are not independent users of public transportation, do not navigate well in unfamiliar surroundings, and don't drive, the family might absorb the burden of transportation to class. Issues such as curfews, dating, drinking, and even laundry, impact everyone in the family and are to be negotiated by everyone in advance if this is going to work.

Many students, clinicians, and counselors worry that commuting from home will socially isolate the student from the mainstream of campus life. Certainly, this is not a trivial issue, but many commuter campuses have highly specialized services, curricula, and social supports for commuting students. In community colleges – without residence halls, or urban schools with limited residence hall availability – there are many opportunities for the commuting student to make friends and socialize out of school – both in the community and on campus, if the student takes advantage of them.

Further, most residential campuses have offices specifically charged with outreach to commuting students and promoting events meant to draw them into overall campus life. If your student becomes a commuter student, it may be helpful to encourage him to eat meals on campus, study in the library between classes, and exchange emails with peers in class in order to facilitate better interaction and communication with fellow students. Often students themselves must seek out these opportunities, which we know many students on the spectrum will not do. An opportunity to practice these skills with the support and guidance of the familiar team is potentially very useful to the beginning college student with AS, as opposed to being all alone in a residence hall with limited social support.

Finally, many families worry that the commuter experience (especially community colleges) is too easy academically for the intelligent student with AS. This may be the case, making course selection all the more important. However, it is also important not to lose sight of the fact that one or two years of college success can build a solid foundation for a move to a more challenging campus environment later on. For many students, we think that getting the academic piece of college under their belt without the additional stress of residence life is the best decision. Students with exceptional intellect could use this stepping-stone as an incentive to develop skills such as conversational strategies, note taking, and time management.

Further, most residential campuses have offices specifically charged with outreach to commuting students and promoting events meant to draw them into overall campus life.

Nonacademic success can be built into every facet of attending a commuter campus. This may be an opportunity to learn to navigate mass transportation or how to drive a car. Also, coping strategies for getting along with peers can be developed on campus, and independent life skills can be developed at home before moving into the dormitory system. Learning how to be a college student is staged to foster success at each step along the way, rather than risking it all in a premature move away to a school.

Distance From Home

Many students want to move as far away from home as possible after graduating from high school, hoping that this will be the key to solving the social problems that plagued them in high school. Reinventing oneself is a necessary rite of adolescent passage. Parents often optimistically agree with their son or daughter in this respect, hoping that the student will grow and toughen up away from home. However, frequently, increasing the distance from home creates anxiety for the entire family. Parents who thought they would be at ease with their child's ability to function in familiar surroundings can become anxious with the reality of sending their student into a large or unfamiliar environment far from home.

Frequently, increasing the distance from home creates anxiety for the entire family.

We have worked with many students who chose their campuses without any thought of the distance from home or the impact that might have on the transition. Being away from familiar surroundings, food, and people can be a difficult adjustment for any college student, and even more so for a student on the spectrum. Add to this the difference in support people, difficult academics, and a total change in schedule … for some students, all these changes are just too much. Distance from home is a very important factor in building a successful transition and must be carefully considered for each individual student.

If commuting to a local school is not a choice, choosing a campus close to home is often a good alternative. Living a comfortable distance (defined as far enough from family so they cannot go home every night but can go home for a weekend) allows students to de-stress, do laundry, or enjoy the company of the family dog. One student greatly appreciated the swing set in his backyard on a semi-regular basis. In this scenario, the student may also still access important supports such as therapists and doctors who are familiar. Such clinicians can help the student learn to cope with the academic and other demands of college by maintaining regular contact and appointments.

Attending college in a familiar town may reduce the novelty of adjusting to a new environment, which can be especially troubling for the student with significant spatial or visual difficulties. No need for a new wardrobe to adjust to an unfamiliar climate; no need to manage an airport or negotiate a ride home over a long distance with a stranger.

Distance from home is a very important factor in building a successful transition and must be carefully considered for each individual student.

We have found that many students who begin at a college close to home (whether at a community college while living at home or a local college in residence) are better prepared to move on – whether taking up residence at the same campus or transferring to a residential college farther away. Whichever choice a family makes, it has also been our experience that when students choose to live close to home, it is extremely important that parents allow them to develop their independence as part of the staged transition. For example, after a short period of time to get used to the laundry facilities on campus, parents may gradually discourage the practice of bringing laundry home.

Somewhat related to the issue of distance is weighing an urban versus a suburban or more rural setting. As parents, we may envision a safe country or suburban campus far from the dangers of the big city. Parents may feel safer with their students in the country setting, fearing that poor judgment might lead the student into trouble in a larger, urban setting. However, young people see it very differently. Sometimes they are correct! For example, the mass transportation options on an urban campus may be far better for the student who does not drive. On the other hand, the hustle and bustle, noise, and smells of the city would be a constant sensory assault. For this student a suburban or rural environment might be a better option. Certainly, an environment close to what the student grew up in may be the most familiar, comfortable, and appropriate choice.

After three weeks, Andrew is feeling overwhelmed with his choice of a large university. In high school his parents, teachers, and counselors all worked as a team guiding him and keeping him motivated. They figured out ways to intercede with his teachers and alter his assignments so that the demands would not stress him out. At college, he doesn't know who will do those things for him.

He received a huge packet during the summer freshman orientation, and his mother helped him select some activities for the fall. But now that he is on campus, he can't find the buildings where the activities are located. He forgot to go online to take his placement tests, so he could not register for the right English or math classes. He had a minor meltdown and refused to participate in a "trust walk" activity set up by staff in his residence hall. His clothes are dirty, and he is afraid to go to the laundry room for fear he will lock himself out of his room. He can't wait to go home.

Large or Small School

Many parents automatically believe that smaller environments are more protective, and thus more desirable for students with AS. Students, on the other hand, may prefer the anonymity of a larger school. This is a perennial debate when considering colleges for students with AS: a small school where students may have more direct contact with faculty and administrators or a larger school where students can move more invisibly with less noticeable quirks.

In the following sections, we will look at the pros and cons of each option.

Larger Schools

A larger school offers a degree of anonymity that many students with AS desire (especially, if they come from a high school where everyone knew them as the "oddball"). A larger campus with more students is naturally more diverse, with generally greater acceptance of fringe or unusual students. By the same token, a larger school may provide a wider variety of people and peers, giving students greater opportunity to find others interested in the same intellectual or recreational pursuits. The student who is passionate about train schedules may find an urban studies major with a cadre of similarly interested students and faculty. The student interested in an arcane variety of anime cartoons might find a late-night viewing partner or even a club. Such a variety of people may improve chances of developing peer relationships simply due to the odds of encountering more students and more tolerance of differences.

While not always the case, larger schools often have larger offices of student support with staff that have had more experience transitioning students with AS. On larger campuses the office of Disability Services (more on this in Chapter 8) is usually freestanding, well staffed, and familiar with a wide range of conditions due to the large number of students served. This can be extremely important in finding service providers whom the family and student trust.

In addition, larger schools typically offer a much wider choice of courses, major areas of study, academic opportunities, and faculty experience. On the other hand, class size may be larger, advising may be difficult to secure, and faculty may be less available to students (especially beginning undergraduates) as most will be taking the standard general education requirements and not get into their major courses with more access to their major advisor, until junior year. Narrow areas of interest, which are prevalent in students with AS, however, can be shaped into majors that might be found on a larger campus but not on a smaller campus.

Students and families should be aware that along with anonymity and a wider degree of opportunities may come isolation as students struggle to find their way amidst the masses. But once a student has adjusted to this environment, we feel that the benefits of life on a larger campus for a student with AS often far outweigh the drawbacks.

A larger school may provide a wider variety of people and peers, giving students greater opportunity to find others interested in the same intellectual or recreational pursuits.

Smaller Schools

Smaller institutions may offer students a greater opportunity to work with service providers who will get to know the students and their accommodation needs on an intimate basis. Faculty and staff also usually interact more at a small school, and students may feel more personally guided. Students often feel more supported and more "known" at smaller schools.

As discussed above, families and parents often feel that smaller environments offer more safety. However, not all students like this feeling. The sense of being the only one like them may be more prevalent on the smaller versus larger campus. Many students feel they're in a fishbowl and that everyone sees them as different. Further, smaller schools may not offer the breadth or depth of experience in dealing with students with AS. Offices of student support may be smaller with more overlapping roles. For example, the director of Disability Services may be a professor of psychology rather than a full-time Disability Services provider.

In summary, the choice of a large versus a small school is very individual. While smaller schools may offer less chaos and more individual support,

Faculty and staff also usually interact more at a small school, and students may feel more personally guided.

keep in mind that with less chaos may come fewer choices. Choice of majors and academic specialization may be restricted, libraries and research facilities may be smaller, and recreational opportunities may be more limited. For some students this is not a liability.

Key Benefits of Various Types of College Environments	
A residential college can provide the student the opportunity to live amidst a large group of peers of similar age/interest and take on greater self-responsibility.	A commuter college can provide the student the opportunity to live at home and develop academic and self-care skills without the additional stresses of residential life.
A college close to home that permits the student to spend weekends at home can allow for time to de-stress and benefit from comfortable, familiar surroundings.	A college more distant from home can afford the student who is able the opportunity to reinvent himself and possibly shed earlier social problems.
A larger school can offer a degree of anonymity; often a more diverse population; greater range of academic/intellectual pursuits; and a larger cadre of student support services staff.	A smaller school can often offer a student a greater familiarity with service providers and increased interaction between faculty and support staff, which allows for more personalized guidance.

Academic Program of Interest

The "ideal" school should offer courses of study and majors that capture the interest of every student (even if not entirely realistic).

If the student's goals and desires cannot be met academically on a given campus, how can we expect him to maintain the motivation to succeed and produce the effort necessary to do so? We know that students with AS often struggle with maintaining interest and motivation. How can we expect these students to thrive at a campus that does not meet their basic academic wishes and talents?

We know that individuals with AS tenaciously pursue areas in which they are passionately interested – autistic preoccupations, islets of special interest, precocious talents, preoccupations, or pet interests – whatever we call them. We also know that these passions can become academic majors, motivators, and even careers. Several schools have developed majors in computer game development, for example. How can the student who wants to pursue this major thrive in a school that has no idea how to foster such interests? Special interests such as architecture, drafting, music, engineering, climatology, cartography, medieval Irish folk tales, genetic engineering, train schedules, punk rock, gaming, and animé can and have been developed into majors and careers. These interests may require specialized academic programs.

Thoroughly investigating each school's course and degree options is a vital part of the college search. Making contact with individual departments or even professors allows the student with AS a glimpse of how academic life becomes professional life and provides a personal contact that introduces the possibility of an ally, advisor, or mentor. This may foster a more natural transition for the beginning student with AS.

Special Interests and Possible Careers	
Weather	• Meteorology • Working for news on radio or TV • Working for government (NOAA) • Emergency management
Japanese animé	• Art • Languages • Interpreting • Costume design
Video games	• Computers • Software testing • Video editing • Video production
Drawing/cartooning/art	• Technical drawing • Architecture • Landscape design • Textbook illustrator
Math	• Accounting • Computer science • Engineering • Psychometrist
Maps	• Geography • Landscape design
Words, language, reading	• Library science • Law or paralegal • Journalism • Researcher • Coding specialist
Animals	• Vet technician • Working for a zoo, humane society, or wildlife resource center
History/politics	• Government, politics • Campaigning • Historian or archivist • Public service work for towns and cities

Special AS Programs

We are delighted that families can now choose among specially designed AS programs. More and more campuses are developing special services and programs for beginning students with AS. For the reasons outlined earlier, we do not encourage families to make their choices based only on the availability of AS programs. A college might have a very well-designed AS program in a region the student dislikes, or without providing the special course of study the student is most interested in pursuing.

No AS program can succeed with an unhappy or unmotivated student, no matter how well conceptualized the program goals. In addition, special programs are subject to the vagaries of funding, as well as the commitment and interest on the part of the campus administration. Therefore, we believe it is essential to carefully consider the factors discussed above prior to selecting a campus based on special programs. The table below outlines some general models found in many of these programs.

Common Service Models		
Types of AS Programs	Services That May Be Available	Providers
Clinical focus	Counseling, groups, supported living and transportation	Therapists, psychologists, or students. Some are off-campus residential programs with college as an add-on. Often expensive
Social skills focus	Peer or other mentors, social skills groups, social programing (activities)	Professors, grad students, Disability Services
Academic skills	Academic coaching, special courses, tutors	Disability Services offices, tutoring centers, outside agencies. Often fee based
Research based	Treatment, testing, support	Researchers and students
Mixed models	One or more of the above	Often fee based, often external agencies to the college

Many college students with AS require additional services that would be provided by special AS programs, with or without the involvement of other areas of student support or disability services. Some programs are firmly ensconced on regular campuses while others are residential off-campus support programs that negotiate for students to take courses at local colleges. Special programs may be associated with additional fees, often very costly. Such programs may include specialty housing, special advising, counseling or therapy, additional academic accommodations, tutoring, or social skills training.

Others are even more specialized. For example, a program may offer supervised or supported living in a shared house or apartment, assistance with daily life skills, and transportation to a local community college (often for an extra fee).

Typical Services Provided by Fee-Based Programs	
Area	**Assistance Provided**
Independent living skills	Supported apartment living: Meal prep/grocery shopping Laundry Cleaning Budgeting/managing money
Academic	Study skills Time management Tutoring Check-ins with instructors Advising
Social skills	Relationship development Communal living Conflict management Friendships and dating
Health/wellness	Exercise and recreation Healthy lifestyle choices Mental health, meds management Stress management Sensory integration
Careers/employment	Internships Mentors Interviewing skills Career exploration

The following checklist is helpful as families search for and select the best college for their son or daughter with AS.

AS Program Checklist for Parents

☐ The program is available in support of the course of study that my child is most interested in pursuing.

☐ The program includes the support my child needs (i.e., specialty housing, academic advising, counseling or therapy, additional academic accommodations, tutoring and/or social skills training).

☐ The program is part of a larger campus supportive of my child's needs.

☐ The program has a track record of success with students with AS and similar challenges.

☐ The staff members' qualifications and experience is available to me.

☐ The program clearly articulates what they can and cannot provide.

☐ The program can connect us with other families to talk to about their experiences.

☐ The program has options for levels of support if my student's needs change.

For some students, special AS programs are the best choice. Other students resist labeling and special programming and will not take advantage of the offered supports. It is important to be sure the campus is supportive, regardless of whether the student chooses to partake of the AS programming or not. It is also important for families to be aware that this is new territory, with very little critical evaluation to date on the effectiveness of college programming for students with AS. We advise families to carefully investigate the track records of success, including the professional and non-professional training and staffing of postsecondary AS programs prior to choosing them.

Molly and her family have been researching colleges for what seems like the past decade. Based on Molly's level of independence and her parents' comfort level, they have decided that she is not yet ready to move away from home. There is a large university in the next county and a smaller community college in Molly's hometown that has an excellent reputation for working with students with learning disabilities. Molly has decided to look at both. She and her parents met with representatives from Student Affairs and Disability Services in both schools and are a little nervous that neither seems to have a good understanding of AS. Nevertheless, the smaller school has seasoned Disability Services professionals who are willing to learn how to support Molly. Important, there is a rapid transit system that can deliver her to campus in under an hour. Finally, the choice of community college gives Molly an excellent opportunity to transfer into the larger state university after two years if she feels ready. Based on these circumstances, they are set to apply.

CHAPTER 3

Applying for Admission

Eric has met with his guidance counselor and has chosen several colleges he thinks he could get into. He would be a first-generation student, whose parents have never sent a child to college. He has been to some websites and has sent for some admissions packets, but he is really not sure how to go about filling out all of the information. Can his tutor write his letters of recommendation? Should he mention that he has a disability? What should he do about the fact that there are several missing classes and not-so-stellar grades on his "permanent record"? The suggested essay topics are too boring, so he plans instead to write a treatise about the flaws in the public transportation system in his hometown.

The process of applying to college is full of mysteries and myths. The process seems fraught with so much more stress than many of us remember when we applied. We hear talks of how competitive it is and of smart kids not getting into any colleges, let alone their college of choice. There are great schools for kids who are committed, but the family may need to be flexible. In this chapter, we will lay out some strategies for applying to these schools and dealing with such things as interviews, writing the college essay, and disclosing the disability.

The Process

Having investigated and selected a range of colleges to apply to, the next step is to figure out what the application should look like, including choice of essay topics, disclosure, and how to handle interviews. As above, we suggest the entire team be involved in these decisions. To review the process for parents who either forgot or are unfamiliar with the admissions process, it typically involves several steps:

1. Meet with school counselor to draw up list of schools that might be appropriate given the student's grades, class ranking, test scores (SAT or ACT) and interests.
2. Visit campuses; look online to refine the choice.
3. Obtain application materials from each relevant school (often on a common application that allows simultaneous application to multiple schools using the same application). Making application involves completing a packet of forms, including listing of personal information, requests for letters of recommendation, transcripts, and a form for the personal essay.
4. Complete application materials and submit by the deadline!
5. Separately arrange for test score reports to be sent to schools.
6. If interviews are part of the process, make proper preparation and complete interview (more below).
7. Sit back and enjoy the wait!

To Disclose or Not to Disclose

When students decide to apply to college, one question comes up early and is sure to generate a great deal of anxiety: Whether to disclose status as a student with AS. Let's explore this frequently asked question right at the outset.

Many students with AS are academically gifted and could get into the college(s) of their choice. Some of these students have achieved academic excellence with extensive supports, while some have received little support in high school. Regardless of the degree of support needed, families question whether it is in a student's best interest to disclose the student's disability status to the office of admissions. Many families worry that disclosing a disability automatically means being rejected. This worry is often fostered by well-meaning guidance counselors and clinicians who have trained families to be wary of disclosure. Indeed, many families are told, "If you tell them, he won't get in."

Regardless of the degree of support needed, families question whether it is in a student's best interest to disclose the student's disability status to the office of admissions.

Rejecting an applicant solely on the basis of disclosure of disability is illegal according to the Americans With Disabilities Act of 1990, amended 2009, 2011. Therefore, if an institution were to reject an applicant due to disability disclosure, this would not be overtly stated as such. Nevertheless, many worry about covert bias in the admissions process.

We have faith in the admissions process, and have worked with many well-trained and honorable admissions professionals who would not engage in any kind of questionable behavior with regard to disclosure. In this connection, however, we add our strong feeling that any college that would behave in such a manner is unlikely to provide any of the supports a student with a disability would need to be successful.

The issue of disclosure is highly personal. Disclosing disability upon application is not required except when applying to special programs that have separate admissions tracks for students with disabilities. You will know those programs when you select them, because they will advertise that they have special admissions considerations (such as submission of testing per special requirements). For all other institutions of higher education, disclosure is entirely a matter of personal choice.

Our experience is that when a student is otherwise competitive with the applicant pool at a given college for a given year, little is gained by disclosure. Families must understand that the admissions requirements are usually not waived or modified based on disclosure of disability. Students with AS are expected to bring admissions portfolios that are equivalent to the typical applicant pool. However, when there are special circumstances that bear explanation, students and their families should consider disclosure.

We have faith in the admissions process, and have worked with many well-trained and honorable admissions professionals who would not engage in any kind of questionable behavior with regard to disclosure.

For example, colleges look for and expect to see certain courses in high school, often without exception (science, math, and foreign language, to name a few), along with evidence of participation in civic activities, sports or other extracurricular activities, and perhaps some period of employment (paid or volunteer). Test scores are expected to fall within a given range depending on the competitiveness of the school. College admissions lore is replete with stories of exceptional students who have it all. While that is not the norm (really!), most students bring more to the table than grades alone. Where does that leave our applicant with AS?

Sometimes our students have been granted waivers on certain courses like math or language (*never* a good idea for a college-bound student) or have not been encouraged or interested in joining any activities outside of school hours. Many have never worked, left home for trips or overnight experiences, or functioned independently. For some

Students with AS are expected to bring admissions portfolios that are equivalent to the typical applicant pool.

students, making it through school has been about all they could manage, what with special appointments, such as OT, speech, and tutoring, which has not left much room for extracurricular activities. We believe it is best to put such circumstances in context within the application rather than allowing the admissions committee to come to their own conclusion about the student's motivation or capability. Different profiles bear explanation, and in such circumstances students and their families should strongly consider disclosure.

Many students choose not to disclose at admissions, and this is fine. Many adolescents are invested in either denying they are a person with a disability, or hope it will go away in a new environment. Others are sick of being seen as different and choose not to formally admit it on their application. This is especially true for the highest functioning students who have had mainstream high school experiences. If this is your student's choice, consider whether she would consent to have a guidance counselor write to address her status as a student with a disability to put a nonstandard admissions application into context. The following vignette highlights this.

Alicia is a student with a mismatch between her grades, extracurricular activities, and College Board scores. Her latest testing showed academic functioning in the superior range and, as a result, she was unable to secure accommodations for the SAT. In addition, she began medication for anxiety during the second half of 10th grade, which greatly improved her focus in class and her grades. She has never joined clubs or sports, and every afternoon has revolved around her pets, tutoring sessions, and various therapeutic supports rather than extracurricular activities. This may not be a very promising admissions portfolio.

Alicia and her family chose to disclose her special needs to the colleges to which she applied rather than risk appearing like an applicant who is neither qualified nor motivated to succeed. Alicia focused her college essay on her love of animals as well as her struggle with AS. She researched carefully and edited with assistance. She was prepared to discuss her journey on all of her interviews, and rehearsed extensively with her therapist, guidance counselor, and parents.

Disclosing in an Essay

Many students with disabilities choose to write their college essays about their individual journeys. This is no different for students with AS. Many feel that theirs is a unique perspective, one that will make their application stand out as being different. This is also a valuable opportunity for a student to describe her experiences in her own words.

However, as the number of applicants with AS increases, college admissions counselors are familiar with these types of essays – thus, the novelty has worn off. What will make a student special?

Be sure to strike an upbeat and positive tone rather than implicitly blaming a school district or exam agency ("I would have scored higher but could not get extra time" or "we found out too late we could get other supports," etc.). Admission staff want to hear how a student with a disability is prepared to address his challenges in adult life,

Unless your student is applying to a special program, you typically do not send documentation of AS to the admissions office.

not how she struggled as a child. How did she use her earlier experiences to learn and change? Encourage the student to keep this in mind as she writes.

What About the Documentation?

Unless your student is applying to a special program, you typically do not send documentation of AS to the admissions office, which is typically neither qualified nor prepared to evaluate test data, read IEP goals, or understand the process. If special classes and programming have been part of high school, it is far better to address this separately in a letter from a school official that clarifies the nature of the services (see recommendation above). Remember that it is absolutely voluntary to do this, and you and your student must decide whether disclosure will be in the student's best interests. Often the Disability Services staff is prepared to have this discussion with regard to their individual campus.

We have been asked many times if an expert can review the documentation during the admissions process. We remind parents that, unless their student is applying to a special program that has a separate admissions track for students with disabilities, admissions offices are not staffed by disability experts and are not required to seek outside assistance. Some schools consult with members of the

Disability Services office when a student with a disability disclos-es. Assistance may also be sought from other campus personnel with regard to how to interpret an applicant who has disclosed AS, especially, if the college is relatively inexperienced with this or if a parent has called to ask specific information. When this is the case, assistance is usually provided to the admissions office and the "ex-pert" is not acting as an advocate for an individual applicant. How-ever, this is not always the case, and you are well advised to check each school separately. *All schools do not approach admissions in the same manner.*

Situations That May Warrant Disclosure

- Grades and test score mismatch
- Variability from year to year or semester to semester attribut-able to changes in clinical status or treatment
- Lack of extracurricular activities
- Waiver of required courses (such as foreign language or math) or other deviation from expected college prep courses
- Attendance in a special program or school
- Absences from school or periods out of school (may include home schooling)
- An interview is recommended or required and student demon-strates unusual speech or interaction features
- Student believes AS is an important part of herself that she wishes to share (we think this is one of the best reasons)

Even if the student chooses not to disclose upon application, we believe it is important for the family to make contact with the Dis-ability Services office at each school to which they apply to dis-cuss any special services, supports, documentation guidelines, or other information specific to this population of students. We also strongly believe that families who choose not to disclose because their son or daughter has done well in high school with little support should consider formal disclosure to the college of choice. We will discuss formal disclosure in Chapter 7 on working with Disability Services.

The Interview

Let's move now to the next, more stressful, aspect of applying to college – the interview! This used to be a major part of the process; however, as the number of applicants has increased and the range of colleges to which they apply has widened across the continent, many campuses have de-emphasized personal interviews as part of the admissions process.

Some schools conduct interviews in the student's hometown with an alum or a travelling member of the admissions office. This may be preferable because it can be conducted in a more familiar environment. Many campuses offer group interviews, which could either be a good thing or a bad thing for a student with AS. Some students shine in a group situation, especially if they have been coached, but most students with AS do better one-on-one than in an unfamiliar group of teens all dressed to impress.

Finally, some campuses still recommend (or even require) a personal interview on campus. If possible, it is often preferable to get a private interview because group interviews can be intimidating for students with AS. This would be considered an accommodation that you do have the right to request. If the campus has an option for interview, carefully consider it. Many students with AS are good ambassadors for themselves and are happy to talk to "adults" about their interests and struggles. Many students have been on stage and are very comfortable "performing" in this manner. Be careful to consult a college counselor about typical college interviews and coach the student well. Role-plays, rehearsal, and scripting are all useful tools in prepping a student for an interview. Anything that renders the situation more familiar and predictable will assist the student. Students should be encouraged to prepare a narrative, and try to stick to that outline as much as possible.

If possible, it is often preferable to get a private interview because group interviews can be intimidating for students with AS.

Certainly, disclosing the presence of AS is important if there is anything about the student that would stand out to the interviewer, such as unusual vocal patterns, avoidance of eye contact, or physical appearance. Giving the student some words to use in describing his or her AS is useful, and many families opt for using the increasingly familiar, albeit soon-to-be-obsolete "Asperger" label simply for its name recognition.

Students should be advised to dress comfortably – if they will be uncomfortable in a tie to the point that they will be distracted or worse, it is best to dress neatly but comfortably. Handshakes and eye contact should be rehearsed as much as possible, and the student should be coached that this is an expected part of the process. Arriving early and getting the lay of the land may also reduce anxiety. And parents please understand that this interview is not necessarily intended to be a shared experience. If a group interview is required and your student simply cannot manage that, it is acceptable to call the admissions office, disclose the situation, and request an individual interview as an accommodation to the admissions process.

The following checklist can guide your thinking and preparation for the college interview.

Admission Interview Checklist

- ☐ Consult the college counselor about the typical college interview and coach the student.

- ☐ Role-play and rehearse in preparation for the interview.

- ☐ Prepare the script or narrative in advance of the interview – and stick to it as much as possible.

- ☐ Consider disclosing the nature of the student's AS if there are any unusual speech or interaction features that would stand out to the interviewer.

- ☐ Dress neat and comfortably. Do not dress in attire that would be a distraction for the student.

- ☐ Practice handshakes and eye contact.

- ☐ Reduce anxiety by arriving early or checking out the environs in advance.

- ☐ Inquire about alternate arrangements to a group interview (if one is required) if this type of interview is not suitable to the student's abilities.

Students with AS can and do get into great schools! In the next chapter, we will begin to outline steps your family will consider as you prepare your young adult to be a college student. As was likely the case when you prepped your child for middle school, camp, or high school, this entails gathering information, trying to anticipate "pressure points," and giving your young adult the tools she or he will need to master this new environment. At this juncture, you will also be building a relationship with key offices on your campus of choice, most particularly with various offices within Student Affairs.

Andrew and his parents anxiously waited for responses to his applications. Will it be a fat envelope or a thin one? Andrew applied to a range of campuses, none of which had a special AS program, but all of which had substantial prior experience with students on the spectrum. He was accepted to their top choice – the large university about three hours' drive from home. Andrew hopes to live on campus, which makes his parents nervous. They are ready to begin the next stage of the transition process.

CHAPTER 4

Getting Your Student to Campus

 Miles' mom drives him to school each day. He has a cell phone that direct dials his mom when classes are over so she can pick him up. He registered for three random classes for his first semester at a medium-sized college close to home. He was confused about what buildings they were in and arrived late for each one the first two weeks. He didn't care that everyone looked at him as he dropped his book bag, but he has noticed that no one talks to him in class, or anywhere on campus, for that matter. He does not know the teachers' names and has not purchased the planner his mentor suggested for recording his assignments. He has the course books that his mother bought online for him, but he does not know what readings are due when, and does not know there is a placement quiz in math in one week. He brings his favorite lunch in a bag and eats on the steps near the location where his mother drops him off and picks him up. He does not know what he will do when it gets cold, maybe sit in the lobby? He has not met the Disability Services staff although his freshman advisor suggested that he do so if he needs extra time for tests. The other kids all look so cool; they know how to act and where to go. Miles wishes he knew how they all got to be friends. He wants to be at college like the other kids on his block, but it is so confusing.

All the uncertainties about moving from high school to college are amplified for the student with AS who is leaving a familiar environment for one that is radically different. In this chapter, we will discuss some important changes your student and your family will go through in the months leading up to leaving for college. Much of this is a shift in how you think about your student and how the student must come to think about him- or herself. For all intents and purposes, the student is now considered an adult!

We will discuss some planning steps that families might consider to familiarize their student with their chosen campus and what to expect. Remember when you previewed kindergarten? Use those same skills to figure out how to make the unknown of college more familiar to your student. And don't be afraid to ask for assistance. Such areas as freshman orientation, how to register for classes, how to find things like washing facilities, doctors, and classrooms will all be novel and scary unless you begin to map them out before the student arrives.

In the Year Before the Student Arrives on Campus

Much of the work of transitioning the student with AS from high school to college is best done before the student attends the first day of classes. As discussed in Chapter 1, ideally, this should begin at least two years before college through a combination of activities of daily living preparation at home beginning at least in middle school, working towards independence through the high school IEP, and building a solid transition-from-high-school-to-college plan into the IEP beginning at least in the start of the junior year of high school. Although the Americans With Disabilities Act obligates high schools to create a transition plan for all graduating students with an IEP, unfortunately far too many high schools give the transition plan very little time or attention. Thus, there may be high hopes but no plan when the student graduates from high school.

Unfortunately, the vast majority of high school special education and guidance departments are generally uninformed about the level of independence and self-advocacy that will be demanded by colleges – after all, their focus is providing the supports necessary for successful graduation from high school. Sadly, all too often special education and guidance departments do not recognize the importance of understanding the basis upon which support services are provided to students with disabilities at the college level or what colleges and universities require of students with regard to documentation, self-advocacy skills, and independent living. Or, the staffing of the guidance and special education are such that they cannot possibly include transition and college information into their already overwhelming jobs. Consequently, unless the student comes from a well-informed and enlightened high school, much of the work of transitioning the student with AS from high school to college is best coordinated by the parents before the student attends the first day of classes.

This work involves the student, his or her parents, the Disability Services professional, and other professionals on campus or in the student's support network, as necessary. We outline some transition strategies in this section. It is important to reaffirm that many of these strategies fall beyond the traditional role of Disability Services and are not mandated under law. We suggest that the family engage in collaboration between the student and the Disability Services office in order to best accomplish these goals. Please see New Student Resource Guide below.

New Student Resource Guide			
Contact:	**Ph/Email:**	**Office:**	**Meeting dates/ time, office hrs.:**
Disability Services Counselor			
Instructors/T.A.s			
Writing Center			
Math Center			
Health Center			
Counselors/Psy.			

New Student Resource Guide			
Contact:	**Ph/Email:**	**Office:**	**Meeting dates/ time, office hrs.:**
Other Support Network			
Advisor Dining Hall Hours; Off-Campus Place to Eat			
Barber or Salon			
ATM Machine			
Residence Advisor Dorm Hours/ Curfew			
Roommates			

We suggest several transition techniques for use in the months before the start of the first term. Guidance counselors can begin the transition process through discussions with students that focus on their concerns and fears and conversations about what they can expect to find on the college campus. Such conversations can begin as early as the first year of high school for students who are anxious about college.

One of the authors' high school-aged son was so worried about "how college students eat" that he declared he could never go to college! It never occurred to him that colleges have dining halls and that he already knew how to navigate such a setting from experiences with the high school cafeteria. Students who will be living in the residence halls can use their penchant for gathering information to research the changes they can expect to find as a dorm resident with their guidance counselor, special education teacher, or mentor.

Become Familiar With and Practice Student Rights and Responsibilities

Under the law, students with disabilities have the right to equal access to all university programs and activities. Other rights that the universities must recognize include the right to receive effective, appropriate, and reasonable accommodations. This is often the first point of intersection between the student with AS and the university, as the student and/or his family contact the university to arrange accommodations for tests or residence hall assignments.

Along with these student rights, however, come students' responsibilities to play an active role in launching the provision of accommodations in keeping with the institution's policies and procedures. In other words, the students must assume the roles that were previously played by their parents and the special education providers in their schools. This can be a daunting task, especially given some of the organizational, communication and social skill challenges of students with AS.

In high school, the special education department takes responsibility for coordinating services, notifying teachers about necessary modifications and accommodations, and monitoring that services are being provided appropriately. At the college level, students are ultimately responsible for self-disclosing their disability to the designated entity on campus and then requesting appropriate supports and services.

The students must assume the roles that were previously played by their parents and the special education providers in their schools.

For example, in high school a student may have received extra time on exams, a note taker, and study guides from the teacher's notes. In college, the student herself must request the accommodations she thinks she will need. Disability Services will then determine if the request is appropriate and negotiate with the student (not the parent). As mentioned, students are ultimately responsible for self-disclosing their disability to the designated entity on campus. Failure to do so means that the university is not obligated to recognize the student as having a disability or offer the legal protection that is afforded. Self-disclosure includes providing documentation of disability in compliance with campus policy.

The student is responsible for requesting her own accommodations and monitoring their effectiveness. Finally, the student must follow established policies and procedures with regard to disabilities accommodations, and must meet required academic and behavioral standards (e.g., be otherwise qualified). For example, if a college requires that students request accommodations the first week of classes and schedule exams one week in advance, it is the student's responsibility to meet these deadlines. Schools do not have to change these general policies for students who have difficulty with scheduling or time management.

Self-Advocacy

Learning to self-advocate is a crucial skill students with AS must be taught in order to become independent. They need to be able to speak up for themselves, describe their needs, and ask for help when necessary. Learning this skill should begin in middle school with the student taking on increased responsibilities at home and in school such as working directly with teachers to arrange accommodations instead of waiting for the resource teacher or making their own arrangements for extracurricular activities, getting together with friends, etc.

Students whose parents and teachers have assumed the advocacy role face their new-found independence during first semester freshman year with added challenges, as they will need to assume increased responsibility for their accommodations each semester.

Other areas to review include the student's level of self-knowledge and disability-specific information. Has she discussed her disability with anyone in the past? If not, the family should review the following with the student:

1. What is in the documentation (including test scores and diagnoses)?

2. What are the functional limitations that accompany the diagnosis or how does your diagnosis effect you and how will it effect your life at college?

3. What are the accommodations and supports requested? (What do you need in each of your classes and is that request supported in your documentation?)

These are the kind of questions Disability Services will ask the student, and the student (not the parent!) needs to be able to work with the support person to come up with appropriate accommodations.

Having to tell their son or daughter the medical diagnosis of disability is an area that gives many parents pause. Somehow they believe that it will make the student feel badly about himself or herself. We firmly believe that knowledge of one's disability

Learning to self-advocate is a crucial skill students with AS must be taught in order to become independent.

gives one understanding and that knowledge is power in this regard. How can a student successfully manage his disability if he doesn't even know its name?

The staff at the Disability Office should not be the first persons of authority to discuss with the student that she has been diagnosed with AS. (As professionals, all of us have had this uncomfortable discussion with students who have repeatedly been told that they do not have AS, when it is abundantly clear from their documentation that they do – one of us even encountered an instance in which the diagnosis was never revealed to the student until after he was dropped off at school.)

In cases where parents have not had a heart-to-heart talk with their student earlier, it is vital that these conversations take place before the student begins college. Parents should understand that the staff at Disability Services cannot withhold this information from adult students. There are a great many books on the market written by young adults about their experiences and thoughts as students on the spectrum, and these can serve as excellent tools to help students learn how to talk about themselves with disability service staff. See for example, *Beyond the Wall* by Stephen Shore, *Born on the Wrong Planet* by Erika Hammerschmidt, and *Aquamarine Blue 5* by Dawn Prince-Hughes in the Recommended Readings section.

Nope, not going to that special ed. office, no way! Luke is so tired of being "special ed. kid." All the kids at his school always knew he took the short bus and that he got special treatment when it was time to take the statewide exams. It was sort of OK when he was younger, but it got embarrassing in high school! Now he is going off to college, and this is a chance for a fresh start. No one knows what he was like in high school. So long as he stays out of Disability Services, all that stigma attached to special ed. will go away ... no more disability, no more AS.

Build Self-Advocacy and General Responsibility Goals Into the IEP

For a student who is college bound, we hope that as early as middle school the transition team included advocacy skills, organizational strategies, and classroom preparation as part of the goals of the program plan. Goals are tailored to the needs and skills level of each individual, and the following suggestions should not be taken as literal. Specific and attainable goals might include the following.

Goals Related to Self-Advocacy and Independence

1. Attendance and participation in team meetings in which the student articulates his disability, strengths, and needs

2. Creation and use of time management system for class assignments and out of class activities

3. Classroom accommodations to be negotiated directly with teachers rather than pull-outs to resource room

4. Increasing independence at home, as reflected by learning to use currency, open a bank account, and take mass transit to and from school or a therapeutic or social activity

5. Independence in activities of daily living, including food preparation, laundry, and personal care

6. Making student responsible for managing and being accountable for free time and academic demands

Disability Services professionals usually insist that the college student with a disability is now an adult who must advocate for himself without parental intervention. This letter-of-the law interpretation is correct; however, we believe that an active partnership between the campus, the family, and the student is a better practice for supporting students with AS as they begin college (with appropriate releases from the student, of course). For example, preparing such materials as discussed in the section above can be a shared task between the Disability Services office and the student's family (who usually know best what the student is most interested in learning about).

Social and Independent Living Skills

Academics are only part of the total college experience. Consistent with the developmental goals of adulthood, students must develop independent living skills as they move away from home. First-year college students must learn to interact with a wide range of people on campus, including professors, administrators, staff, and peers. They must also learn to interact as adults rather than adolescents in such areas as dating, sexuality, and parties (including dealing with peer pressures around alcohol and drugs). They are called on to behave according to student conduct codes that provide strict guidelines for campus behavior in class and in residences and are rarely forgiving based on a student's status as a person with a disability. Students who are found in violation of student behavioral standards are subject to judicial review and sanction and are not protected because they have a disability. We will discuss this further in Chapter 5 on laws families need to know.

73

Unlike secondary school teachers and staff, college faculty are not told that a particular student has AS, nor are faculty and staff routinely notified of the student's diagnosis, learning preferences, habits, and so forth. Indeed, college faculty typically are asked to provide accommodations without knowing any specifics about the student's disability since the Disability Services offices is prohibited by law from disclosing diagnostic information without students' explicit permission to do so. Thus, faculty members may receive an email or letter from Disability Services requiring that a given student be given extended time on exams and a separate room. The faculty member is not informed of why this is necessary, only that he or she must provide the accommodation. Similarly, residence hall staff may not know about a student's AS or sensory difficulties until, and unless, they are told specifically by the student and her family.

Families often believe that the information on the medical forms that they complete prior to enrollment will be distilled and transmitted to all persons working with or encountering their student on campus. This is not the case. Therefore, families need to understand that the student must set the boundaries in terms of what will and will not be disclosed and to whom. For example, a student may want his lab instructor to know about a condition or medication that causes his hands to shake, and, therefore, can make it difficult to perform certain fine-motor activities, but there is no need for a faculty member in a lecture class to be informed of this condition.

Scheduling and Time Management

Most high school students receive little or no training in planning, scheduling, and time management. Despite their well-known problems in this area, students on the autism spectrum are even less prepared for how to manage time or meet deadlines for things like housing lotteries, registration, or long-term projects. If your student had extensive in-school support, homework helpers, coaches, or parental assistance, he is likely underprepared to manage his time independently at college. We have provided some tips to remedy this situation below.

Academics are only part of the total college experience.

Parent Tasks ...

- Quit being the snooze alarm. Invest in an alarm clock
- Help student make own appointments, refill own medications
- Encourage and teach the use of a time management system
- Increase responsibilities and chores at home
- Use of timers rather than reminders from Mom
- Allow natural consequences to actions – even if "uncomfortable" at first
- Obtain help with social skills if not addressed at school
- Realistically assess student's readiness versus demands of a given job or college
- Get current, comprehensive assessment of disability
- Make sure all areas impacted are addressed (depression, anxiety, OCD, ADHD)
- Explore eligibility for Vocational Rehabilitation Services through your state
- Look into federal TRIO Programs (http://www.ed.gov/about/offices/list/ope/trio/index.html). These are programs offered by the U.S. Department of Education designed to motivate and support low-income, disabled, and first-generation college students. Support from middle school through graduate school.

We suggest you start as early as possible to teach the student time management. Families often start with a large wipe-off monthly wall calendar in grade school, recording appointments, planned events, and tasks that need to be done, then shifting to a four-month wipe-off calendar in middle school on which appointments, school events, school calendars, tests, and projects as well as extracurricular and family obligations are recorded.

As the student approaches high school, she should be taught how to use a weekly calendar as well as a daily "to do" list. In high school, the IEP should include acquisition of time-management skills, including how to estimate how long a task takes (i.e., how long it takes to do one math problem and use this information to estimate how long it will take to complete the twelve problems assigned for homework). Armed with this training and reinforced through work with special education staff, teachers, and parents, students will learn how to break down their college syllabi and enter due dates, exam dates, and college deadlines such as housing deposits and course registration. For students who continue to need help and support in this area, general academic support centers on campus are usually very good at teaching these skills, even if they are not AS experts. Personnel within Disability Services may similarly provide this sort of assistance.

When and Where to Get Academic Help

College freshmen who have been successful in high school typically do not know when they are in trouble. This is one of the pitfalls of having an adolescent view of the world.

Students with AS often take great pride in their gifts and are invested in not seeing their academic shortcomings. Students need to learn how to tell when they need help and where to go to get it. Students may not understand that they can ask professors to assess how they are doing in the course compared to their classmates and the course demands. They can ask professors for tutoring, clarification, review of lecture and reading material, and extra help, but probably don't know that their professors usually welcome these requests.

In this chapter we discussed some of the areas in which families need to prepare their son or daughter in the months preceding college. The next chapter will outline some of the changes in the legal landscape relevant to the transition from high school special education laws to civil rights statutes that apply in higher education. Understanding these changes will prepare parents to take a different role in the accommodation process, and enable them to better assist their student to advocate for him- or herself.

Alicia selected a medium-sized residential college in her hometown. She and her family think she can live away from home since she has been to camp before. They had several meetings with Disability Services at her new school in the spring and summer before her arrival. They talked about the sort of residence hall she would need (smaller, one roommate, shared bath) and what sort of meal plan would suit her. She was directed to the appropriate office to make those requests. They also discussed the academic requirements at the school, and she understands that she will have to take an English class. She has arranged (with the help of the Disability Services office) to meet privately with an advisor to register for her classes. She hopes she can register for the course in science fiction. She was anxious about the summer orientation and opted to stay at home rather than in a room shared by four unknown incoming freshman. But she toured her residence hall over the summer and met the RA. Housing has arranged for her to move in one day early. She also has her new roommate's email address but has not yet contacted her. Her therapist and she have a plan to see each other monthly and to email weekly. She is anxious but feels ready.

CHAPTER 5

Laws Families Need to Know

*Molly always had an exemption from foreign lan-
guage. Her IEP in high school was very clear that
she could not learn another language – that was even
confirmed in her neuropsychology evaluation. But she just
had a meeting with her advisor, who told her she has to
register for a foreign language class. These college people
could not make her take a foreign language; it must be
against the law! Isn't it?*

Families are typically unprepared for the fact that having
achieved high school graduation, students with AS now
leave the familiar territory covered by the Individuals With
Disabilities Education Act (IDEA) and enter the realm of
Section 504 of the Rehabilitation Act of 1973 and the Americans With Disabilities Act of 1990. For students who plan to
attend college, the differences are important in terms of planning whether they should extend high school for an additional year and delay graduation and what services are needed (or
possible). In our experience, failing to understand the legal
framework of higher education is the source of much strife
between the college student with a disability, his or her family, evaluator, and members of the professional team.

In this chapter, we will briefly review special education entitlements and the differences college students face under the dual civil rights laws of the ADA and Section 504 of the Rehabilitation Act. We include this information because in our experience, lack of knowledge about this legal shift underlies much of the confusion and unhappiness families face with regard to transitioning their students with disabilities.

IDEA vs. ADA/504

As students with disabilities move forward to higher education, the legal focus shifts from entitlement and remediation to protection from discrimination and equal access. Increasingly, the student must be able to self-identify as a person with a disability and demonstrate that he or she is qualified as a member of a protected group. In other words, adult students are expected to take charge of their own education and their disability. We know that this may come as a shock to many highly involved families who find their function limited by the policies of the university. It can be an unpleasant surprise to discover that documentation guidelines and the review processes for eligibility are more stringent, as the diagnosis alone is no longer the only criterion for receiving services. Students may face for the first time rejection for accommodations and services. This may particularly be the case when symptoms and impairment are relatively mild.

Even when approved, most families will discover that college services and accommodations are usually more limited than what they experienced in high school. For example, aides and social coaches are typically not provided by colleges and universities for qualified undergraduates. We will return to this later in this chapter.

Rather than one special education entitlement act, two civil rights statutes are key in the life of the college student with a disability.

Section 504 of the Rehabilitation Act and the Americans With Disabilities Act are statutes that prohibit discrimination solely on the basis of disability in employment, education, and physical plant, and thus protect individuals with disabilities from discrimination. The key differences between special education laws and disability statutes that protect college students with disabilities are summarized below.

As students with disabilities move forward to higher education, the legal focus shifts from entitlement and remediation to protection from discrimination and equal access.

The Individuals With Disabilities Education Act (IDEA; http://idea.ed.gov)

IDEA is a law ensuring services to children with disabilities throughout the nation. IDEA governs how states and public agencies provide early intervention, special education, and related services to more than 6.5 million eligible infants, toddlers, children and youth with disabilities. As such, this is an entitlement law that ensures that each child, no matter the disability, will be educated in the most successful way possible. All children are entitled to this education through the high school diploma or through age 21.

Section 504 of the Rehabilitation Act of 1973 (http://www.hhs.gov/ocr/504.pdf)

This is a civil rights statute that prohibits discrimination on the basis of disability in programs and activities, public and private, that receive federal financial assistance. This is the law that mandates accommodations in higher education, for the most part. No funding to the student or the campus is associated with this law.

The Americans With Disabilities Act (ADA) (www.ada.gov)
Enacted in 1990 and amended in 2009, this is a federal civil rights law that extends Section 504 to protect against discrimination for reasons related to disability in employment, education, and accommodations. It applies to public and private entities that receive federal funds, and thus covers access in most places of employment, as well as colleges and universities.

Titles II and III of the ADA prohibit discrimination on the basis of disability in employment, government, public accommodations, commercial facilities, transportation, and telecommunications.

Titles II and III of the ADA prohibit discrimination on the basis of disability in employment, government, public accommodations, commercial facilities, transportation, and telecommunications. It includes building and facilities access, employment practices, self-evaluation, and grievances.

The Federal Educational Right and Privacy Act (FERPA) (www.ferpa.gov)
This is a privacy act that originally was enacted to give individuals the right to inspect and amend their educational records. More current interpretation is to protect disclosure of personal student information. Campuses interpret FERPA more or less stringently with regard to contact with parents, disclosure of grades, or even disciplinary actions against their offspring (including suspension and expulsion). One of the main impacts of this act is that it limits the release of student information regarding the presence or nature of a student's disability to others in the campus community. On some campuses, FERPA is so strictly applied that administrators and staff are instructed not to speak to a student's parents without

the student's written consent, except in extreme emergencies (e.g., the student is ill and in the hospital).

The core of these laws is self-disclosure of disability. While students are not obligated to disclose their disability, if they are asking for accommodations or services, they must self-identify to the appropriate office on campus (usually the Disability Services office) and explain their disability and the functional limitations (note that this must be done by the student, not the parents). Once the student has disclosed her disability and provided documentation, the disability eligibility and the merits of the accommodation request are separately reviewed. In practical terms, this means that each accommodation is re-reviewed without consideration of what services and accommodations the student received in high school.

What Is Formal Disclosure?

Formal disclosure is the process by which a student becomes recognized as an individual with a disability by the campus. It is NOT the same as disclosure on the admissions application, nor is it accomplished by filling out medical papers with student health. Colleges interpret privacy laws very strictly, which prevents individual offices within a university from sharing much information. It is common for families to assume that because they shared the student's high school IEP with Admissions and answered the questions on the medical forms sent to student health, they have completed the disclosure process.

The reality is that in order to be protected under the law, your son or daughter needs to be formally recognized as a student with a disability. Specific procedures and policies vary from campus to campus, but most entail the student personally disclosing to the office of Disability Services (variably named), providing medical documentation of disability, and asking for services, accommodations, or support. Families cannot disclose for their sons or daughters. Self-disclosure and self-advocacy are required (although family assistance with the student with AS is common and usually welcome).

A general timeline is presented below for the months leading up to the first day of classes at the chosen university:

Formal disclosure is the process by which a student becomes recognized as an individual with a disability by the campus. It is NOT the same as disclosure on the admissions application.

Sample Timeline		
Spring	**Summer**	**Fall**
Upon being accepted to a school, the student should contact Disability Services to find out how to formally register with the office and request accommodations. Students should also ask if there is a scheduled Open House in which admitted students are invited to visit Disability Services for a tour, to meet the staff, and to get an overview of policies and procedures.	During Orientation: The student should meet with Disability Services and discuss possible course load and any course issues (professors/instructors with accents; time between classes to get to another building; number of classes each day, etc.).	First Week of Classes: The students should meet with Disability Services to discuss accommodations for each course and get notices (letters) for each instructor. Time of continued meetings with Disability Services should be set and any additional services or program meetings should be scheduled.

Sample Pre-Semester Prep

TASK	CONTACT INFO/DETAILS	NOTES	DONE
Contact Disability Services and TRIO. Make initial appt. to discuss accommodations and meeting schedule.	Names: Office Address: Phone:		
Set up your college email. Fwd your personal email to this account.	New email:		
Look up your professors' names and emails. Send email introducing self and requesting early syllabi.	Names: Emails: 1. 1. 2. 2. 3. 3. 4. 4.		
Print each syllabus. Place in plastic sleeve. Color coordinate 3-ring notebooks for each course. Purchase 3 hole punch for new handouts.	Class: Color:		

Sample Pre-Semester Prep

TASK	CONTACT INFO/DETAILS	NOTES	DONE
Look up books required for each course. Buy from bookstore before classes start.	Class: Books not available yet: 1. 2. 3.		
Practice using transportation. Note bus schedules and stops.	Bus info and costs:		
Walk your daily schedule on campus (to each building and classroom)	M,W,F route: Bldings, rm #s T, Th route: Bldings, rm #s:		
Print your weekly schedule. Designate course time on a Weekly Planner. Add reoccurring meetings, meals and wake/sleep times	* See weekly planner		

Sample Pre-Semester Prep			
TASK	CONTACT INFO/DETAILS	NOTES	DONE
Purchase College Planning Guide. Familiarize yourself w/ important dates and resources on campus. Highlight dates.			
Use college website to find info on a club or activity to join. Write meeting dates and contact info on your Resources Guide on back of this handout.	Potential Clubs: Contact: 1. 2. 3.		
Obtain college I.D. card. Explore how to use for debit/ credit or dining hall expenses.	I.D. number: Bank info:		
Other:			
Locate resource for refilling any meds (on campus mental health, etc)			

What Is Documentation?

Documentation is the material that establishes that an individual is a person with a disability; it is the written statement that supports the need for accommodations or other services. It is vital to the accommodation process at all colleges and universities.

Appropriate and current documentation in the postsecondary setting validates continued eligibility to receive accommodations and services based on the student's current level of function in an academic setting. The high school special education plans (IEP or 504 Plan) are not sufficient documentation of a disability for the purposes of accommodations in college. Clear and specific evidence in the documentation that the disorder limits one or more major life activities in an academic setting is essential to access services.

Suggested Components of Documentation

Documentation of AS should …

1. Be prepared by a clinician possessing appropriate credentials, including a psychologist, psychiatrist, neurologist, or developmental pediatrician. Note that documentation submitted by speech-language pathologists or occupational therapists is helpful, but diagnosis should be by credentialed diagnostician.

2. Be typed and signed on professional letterhead with license numbers and state of licensure of person issuing the diagnosis.

3. Include student's complete history (developmental, medical, educational, family).

4. Summarize or include prior assessments as relevant (neuropsychological, psychoeducational, psychiatric, language, etc.).

5. Include current testing such as standardized tests of intelligence or aptitude, academic achievement, and other cognitive processes as relevant (memory, attention, motor, executive functioning, etc.) appropriate to the current age of the individual.

6. Provide summary of standardized test scores.

7. Demonstrate current impairment in a major life activity.

8. Rule out other medical, learning, and psychiatric disorders and explanations for current difficulties.

9. Summarize prior history of accommodations.

10. Formulate clear diagnostic summary utilizing current standard nomenclature.

11. Formulate clear recommendations for accommodations in current setting.

12. Provide objective reason for each requested accommodation.

Under IDEA, the school typically prepares documentation following its assessment of the child. This may or may not contain the results of behavioral evaluations, speech-language evaluations, OT evaluations, neuropsychological testing, teacher observations, etc. While these are not necessarily useful for college documentation, nevertheless consider gathering all information. Many parents have thick files containing all of the assessment reports going back to their child's earliest childhood while others have not retained those copies. Prior to the student leaving high school, it is important that the family gather all relevant documentation from the school records. You never know when it might be needed.

Colleges and universities are permitted to establish reasonable guidelines for what constitutes acceptable documentation of different disability categories. Most have well-reasoned guidelines for documenting attention disorders, learning disabilities, and psychiatric disorders. Few have articulated guidelines for documentation of AS, but some are under consideration. (See www.ets.org/disability for examples of formal documentation guidelines for those conditions.)

We prefer that documentation be in the form of a current, comprehensive neuropsychological evaluation that highlights areas of functional impairment. Students with AS do not typically have "classic" learning disabilities. Thus, testing must go beyond the standard psychoeducational assessment to pinpoint specific areas of weakness that may require accommodation. For example, the need for a note taker or clarification of exam answers may not be clear without testing that targets oral listening skills, working memory, or written language organization. Particularly useful is a thorough evaluation of executive and other self-regulatory skills. Be prepared to provide a recent (usually within three years and utilizing adult-level tests) psychological or neuropsychological assessment. It is important that this contain measures of academic achievement if the student will be requesting academic accommodations such as extra time on tests. Each requested accommodation must be supported by the documentation both objectively (e.g., test score or statement) and as part of the formulation of recommendations. Supplements from older assessments and statements from treating physicians and other professionals are useful in this process.

The transition IEP no longer mandates testing; the former triennial testing under IDEA was eliminated several years ago. Therefore, families and professionals must determine together whether the student will require an update of his documentation and plan for how that will be accomplished. In most cases, the Disability Services staff is happy to discuss this issue with prospective families. Additional documentation by a psychiatrist is often useful to better understand a student's reactions to stress, mitigating measures in terms of anxiety reduction, depression, and so forth.

Other co-existing psychiatric diagnoses, treatment, and response to treatment (especially medications and suicidal thoughts, gestures, or attempts) should be carefully documented for the Disability Services office as well as for the Student Health Center. Psychosocial assessment reports that highlight the student's level of social functioning and friendship patterns, or response to authority can be very useful. Occupational therapy assessments detailing continuing sensory sensitivities may be of great use when understanding residence hall placements or classroom behavior issues.

Documentation and Eligibility

While documentation is a critical part of establishing eligibility under ADA/504, providing documentation of the current condition is only the first step in establishing eligibility for reasonable and appropriate accommodations at the college level. A diagnosis does not necessarily equate with disability, and the Disability Services office will make an independent determination that a student is a qualified student with a disability.

In the same fashion, a disability does not guarantee a particular accommodation. Accommodations are determined by the Disability Services professional not a team, as was the case in high school. Accommodations are individually determined based on the functional limitations of the student's particular disability. Only when a student's limitations in a particular course, (lecture for note-taking accommodations or multiple-choice tests and extra time, etc.) are determined, can accommodations be decided.

Documentation should clearly specify and support your student's eligibility and his need for specific accommodations, Sadly, this

91

level of documentation is not always available to families. We encourage families to provide documentation from earlier clinicians to support the longstanding presence of AS when the current documentation is insufficient.

Families and professionals must determine together whether the student will require an update of his documentation and plan for how that will be accomplished.

Definition of a Disability for Purposes of Documentation and Accommodation

The legal definition of a disability is "a physical or mental impairment that substantially limits one or more major life activities" or something that makes an individual "unable to perform a major life activity, or significantly restricts the condition, manner, or duration under which a major life activity can be performed, in comparison to the average person" (Sect. 504, RA 1973; ADA 1990; Americans With Disabilities Amendment Act, 2009). This definition changed somewhat with the recent amendment to the ADA; however, the basic elements remain unchanged.

Who Is "Qualified"?

Another distinction under ADA/504 that is not present in IDEA is that students are now reviewed to see if they qualify as a student with a disability. In most instances, a diagnosis of AS is considered a disability; however, this is not always the case, especially when the student is very high functioning. This is a very difficult concept for many families to come to terms with.

In addition to documenting a disability, students requesting accommodations in college must show that they are "otherwise qualified" to attend classes and complete required work (meaning that the academic standards of the university are enforced) and maintain appropriate behavioral standards (meaning that the University Conduct Codes are enforced). A final benchmark of being otherwise qualified is that students be able to advocate for themselves with the minimal level of assistance.

What a surprise to be told that your student must now fit the program, with accommodations that are determined by an outside agent (i.e., not the family) to be reasonable and appropriate. Often parents want to continue the special education entitlements in the college setting. Not only does the law not cover this, but the practice is not usually productive in terms of helping students develop independence and self-advocacy skills. (Further details regarding the differences between these laws may be found at http://www.ccdanet.org/differenceschart.html. Also see http://www.hhs.gov/ocr/504.)

This distinction is one of the cruxes of successful transition, as the student and the family are asked to understand that the university does not consider students to have a disability simply because they have been diagnosed with AS. We know it is frustrating to be told that having a diagnosis is not equivalent to having a disability within the meaning of the law. "Otherwise qualified" is not a statement about whether your student is smart enough to go to college. Rather, it refers to whether an individual with a disability is able to conform with campus policies and regulations, such as independently attending classes and completing required work, or complying with conduct codes. In other words, it addresses the question of whether the student is "otherwise qualified" to be a student on campus.

Accommodating Students With Disabilities

The ADA states that colleges and universities must make modifications to ensure that students have access to all programs, facilities, and activities and ensure that students are not discriminated against or excluded solely on the basis of disability. This means that students with disabilities have the right to receive accommodations to mitigate the impact of their disability on their academic performance as part of "leveling the playing field" vis-à-vis students without disabilities. The ADA does not require colleges to create special programs,

In most instances, a diagnosis of AS is considered a disability; however, this is not always the case, especially when the student is very high functioning.

supports, or policies for students with disabilities. Similarly, the law does not require that students do less work, be graded any differently, or in any way be given an unfair advantage over other students. These are difficult ideas to absorb, so we will highlight some of them below.

As part of the accommodation process, colleges expect students who qualify for accommodations to be able to attend classes and complete the required work – academic standards don't change. For example, students will be asked to do the same assignments and will be evaluated using the same academic standards as peers without disabilities. They will be expected to read the same books, write the same sorts of term papers, and attend the same classes as students without a disability. They will be fully mainstreamed as college students.

The Accommodation Process	
Steps to Take	**Person Responsible**
Self-disclose per policy/procedures of campus (usually office of Disability Services)	Student
Provide medical documentation of disability as per policies of individual campuses	Student, family, clinical team
Request specific accommodations and services	Student
Review request to determine if student with a disability qualifies	Disability Services
Determine reasonable accommodations that are appropriate to the disability and is in accordance with the fundamental requirements of school, program, or course	Disability Services
Provide accommodations (will differ per campus)	Disability Services, faculty, student
Continue to develop and practice self-advocacy skills	Student, with Disability Services help

You and your student may also need to get used to the idea that many accommodations he or she used in high school will not be provided at college. Examples of accommodations that are not supported in most higher education settings include personal aides for academics or housing, social coaches, disability-specific content tutoring, and one-to-one assistance for out-of-class work (homework).

Some schools offer specialized programs where these services are offered for a fee. Since federal law does not require services above and beyond academic accommodation, colleges and universities must charge for them in order to deliver the specialized and time-intensive service from highly trained staff.

Students with AS often need academic support in subjects that are not their strength. For example, a student who is strong in math and science but weak in English and humanities may require extended time for tests in the weaker areas and no accommodations in their strength subjects. Extended time, a private room for exams, assistance with organization and time management, and time to discuss questions privately with a professor are all common accommodations for students with AS. Asking to be excused from courses in the weaker area would not be considered a reasonable request, however. Asking for accommodations or support to deal with such weaknesses would be entirely appropriate.

Students with disabilities have the right to receive accommodations to mitigate the impact of their disability on their academic performance as part of "leveling the playing field" vis-à-vis students without disabilities.

Finally, qualified students with disabilities must also be able to maintain appropriate behavioral standards in class. There are no exceptions made to conduct codes for students with AS. This is different from high school, where behaviors that could be explained by AS were usually not punished. For example, an outburst in class or an argument with a professor might lead to conduct code charges. The fact that the student has AS may be brought up and could be part of determining any sanctions to be brought. However, the presence of any disability does not excuse the student's behavior or eliminate the prohibition of disruption of the educational environment. Finally, in this and all other respects, the student with a disability is expected to be able to advocate for himself or herself with minimal outside assistance.

Confidentiality

One final new note: Since your college-aged son or daughter is now legally an adult, he or she has full access to all educational and medical records with full protection of confidentiality. If there are reports you have not previously shared, he or she now has the legal right to see them. Please do not ask the Disability Services office or the health services to withhold information or records – they can't and won't do it. Many colleges do not even send out grades or information such as disciplinary actions. Prepare yourself, and set the rules about what you expect (or even demand) that your student share with you before you pack up the car.

There are no exceptions made to conduct codes for students with AS. This is different from high school, where behaviors that could be explained by AS were usually not punished.

In this chapter, we discussed relevant laws and the challenge involved in parents shifting away from a hard-won skill set that may have helped get your student to college, to less parental involvement as a result of the fact that their college-aged child is legally an adult in the eyes of higher education. We understand that this may be one of the hardest steps in the process!

In the next chapter, we will look at "who's who on campus," which will get you and your student on the same page in terms of understanding who are the important players on campus and outline some especially important offices to get to know.

Molly's high school submitted the official IEP as well as a copy of the partial testing from 10th grade, which concluded that she was a student with high-functioning autism. Prior services included speech, occupational therapy, pull-out resource room, untimed tests, and a full-time classroom aide to assist with transitions. The aide was removed at the beginning of high school. Molly's transition plan stated that she was planning to attend college; however, they determined she did not need to be retested. Wisely, her parents chose to have an independent private evaluation in 11th grade. The neuropsychologist performing the evaluation took the time to summarize the volume of testing results her parents had provided and determined that Molly's reading was significantly slow and her handwriting was illegible. As a result, the recommendations called for copies of professor notes, extra time for exams in a separate room, and use of a computer for tests that required writing.

Disability Services received this material over the summer before Molly started and queried whether there was additional support for separate testing locations. Molly's psychopharamacologist provided a letter discussing the treatment and medications Molly received for significant anxiety symptoms with a further recommendation that she take exams in a separate room. She and her family were satisfied with the substitution of a peer note taker for copies of faculty notes. She has a follow-up appointment with Disability Services for the first week of school to review the process and practice requesting accommodations from her professors.

CHAPTER 6

Getting Familiar With Your College: Who's Who on Campus

Luke is in trouble! He just received notification that he has to meet with the Dean of Students and maybe the judicial board. He has no idea who these people are or why they want to see him, but he thinks it might be related to the shouting match he had with his roommate the other evening. An older-looking student had come into the room to break up the fight, and while he identified himself as the "RA," Luke has no idea what that means. Another person wearing a suit was called in, who the RA referred to as "Mr. John So and So." That guy told Luke he was to report to "Central Admin" the next day, but Luke has no idea what that means either. There is no "Central Admin" on the map he has. He calls his parents, who call the office of the registrar and tells them Luke can't come to the meeting with "John" because he is too busy.

If a successful partnership is to be fostered for the transitioning college student, it is important that everyone in your student's support system understand the "mechanics" of higher education. Recall how your child struggled with the size and newness of middle school? High school? Why would we expect such challenges to magically go away because he got into the college of his choice? How can you help make it more familiar and less meltdown-provoking? So many things to find out together. How is the campus navigated? How complicated is the transportation system? How far apart are the buildings and how far from the residence halls?

Both you and your student will be exposed to unfamiliar people, places, and terminology. Who is the bursar? What does the registrar do? Since the university will expect the student to handle her affairs as an adult, it is important that all of you get acquainted (figuratively, probably not literally) with the major players on campus. That is what this chapter is about.

You can help your student familiarize herself with the divisions of her campus. To the extent that she can commit to memory the hierarchy, she may avoid some predictable pitfalls (such as not calling a dean by his first name unless invited to do so, or calling a professor "mister" instead of "doctor" or "professor").

Much of this is learned by paying attention to what other students do and following their lead. However, due to inherent characteristics, the student with AS may miss these social cues and, therefore, make errors in this new environment.

You can help enormously with this preparation by explaining the new environment to your student and preparing her as best you know how. That may be visually with extra visits to campus with a guide (discussed further in Chapter 7), or however the student best learns new environments. Campus administrations are typically divided into Academic Affairs, Student Affairs, and Business Affairs, all reporting to the office of the president. On smaller campuses, this may be one person rather than an office or department. The general organizational chart below illustrates this hierarchy, although it will vary from college to college.

Typical Organizational Chart

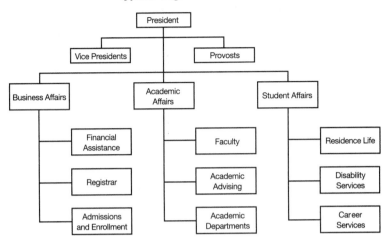

Upper Administration

Usually, the president of the college or university is assisted by a team of vice presidents and assistants. Their office is responsible for all major initiatives at the school, including the overall strategic plan, mission, fund raising, and budget oversight. Most students go their whole careers without meeting the president of their school; others have the opportunity to have him or her as a professor. Also, presidents may be found all over campus, at games, cultural events, etc.

Academic Affairs

The academic side is comprised of the provost as the chief academic officer, assisted by academic deans, who typically manage smaller schools within a large university. These deans oversee academic departments, academic standards, faculty, grants, budgets, and other academic issues in their individual schools. Department chairs do the same for their individual departments, managing the classroom and academic issues encountered by their professors (typically ranked as full, associate, assistant, instructor, fellow, teaching assistant). Faculty advisors may be professors or Student Affairs professionals who provide some level of student support and counseling. Finally, the division of Academic Affairs is assisted in everything they do by a host of clerical, support, and research staff.

Business Affairs

The business side of the organization is comprised of the office of the registrar, which handles such areas as full- or part-time registration, tuition and fees, and leaves of absence. Business Affairs and the office of the bursar (or student accounts) are responsible for finances and may also encompass financial assistance and scholarships. Enrollment and retention, admissions, development, and alumni affairs are also typical offices within the business division of most universities and colleges, each with its own hierarchy of directors, managers, and support personnel.

Student Affairs

Students with AS and their families should become very familiar with the various offices within Student Affairs. This office typically falls under the Dean of Students and may include such areas as Disability Services, Judicial Affairs, Counseling and Wellness, Housing and Residence Life, dining services, tutoring services, and career services. Students need to understand that the offices under the Dean of Students are critical supports as well. Because of the importance in the lives of students with AS, the offices of Disability Services, Residential Life, and Mental Health will be discussed in separate sections later on.

Judicial Affairs

This office is charged with student conduct, discipline, and safety. In addition to enforcing conduct and behavior codes, Judicial Affairs is mandated to ensure that students comply with university conduct codes and policies and respect the rights of others on and off campus. In this regard, Judicial Affairs often works with campus and local law enforcement, housing and residence life staff,

Students with AS and their families should become very familiar with the various offices within Student Affairs.

and academic deans in areas such as noise violations in residence halls, drug and alcohol violations in off-campus parties, plagiarism, and other academic impropriety.

Conduct Codes

Every institution of higher education has a code of conduct by which all students must abide. General behavior such as "students shall not disrupt the educational environment" is standard at every college and university in some form. Students with AS usually do not breach these codes on purpose but may participate in unacceptable behaviors because they do not understand the consequences of their actions. For example, a student may feel the need to correct a professor or continually interrupt lectures to add his personal viewpoint. Many faculty members do not tolerate such disruption and will file a complaint about a "disruptive student."

Disability is not an excuse for breach of conduct code. As students with AS usually appreciate having rules and guidelines, they would benefit from working with someone from Disability Services or the Community Standards office on understanding the rules of academic conduct prior to matriculating on campus.

Make yourself familiar with the academic and other conduct codes on your student's campus and work with your student to understand these as rules that must not be transgressed. Once the student

103

understands the conduct code, he may benefit from direct role-play scenarios to be sure there is a solid understanding of the codes and the consequences for breaking them.

Other Conduct Issues

*   *Stalking and other inappropriate behaviors.* One particular area of concern is stalking. Many students on the spectrum do not realize that when they text repeatedly or lurk outside of classrooms because they are afraid to talk to a girl they may be engaging in this form of risky behavior.

    Campuses do not tolerate "inappropriate contact" or pursuit, which is usually interpreted as stalking. Complaints of strange or unusual behaviors may include students who wander into other students' dorm rooms without recognizing that this is a violation of privacy. Students have been known to hack into computer files or online accounts because they are curious and because they possess the skills to do it. Other complaints include online stalking, which involves repeated texts, emails, or social media postings that the target student finds annoying if not outright threatening.

    It must be made absolutely clear to your student that such behavior is unacceptable! Inappropriate social interaction is often interpreted (incorrectly) as harassment. When someone (male or female) violates personal space or uses inappropriate language, this can lead to accusations of harassment.

    Campuses are not required to take into account any disability-related factors that may have been related to the incident. Your student can and probably will be disciplined for any stalking-related behaviors without regard for his social skills disorder, literalness or rigidity, or lack of understanding of boundaries and social mores. Set your son or daughter up for success by teaching social skills and social boundaries, as needed, before they arrive on campus. See reference list for resources in this area.

When someone (male or female) violates personal space or uses inappropriate language, this can lead to accusations of harassment.

• *Dangerous behavior.* Self-injurious behavior is not common in higher functioning individuals with AS, so it is usually not a problem in college students with AS. However, students sometimes exhibit these behaviors when under severe stress. A full-blown AS meltdown is a dramatic event to witness, as the individual may be temporarily unable to respond rationally to any attempt to calm him down. Students who are prone to extreme reactions may not be ready for the independence college life requires. Students who have demonstrated that they are not safe on campus are typically not ready to be there and may be asked to leave campus housing or, in extreme situations, leave school completely.

Career Services

These offices are important for arranging student internships, field placements and clinics, on-campus jobs, and résumé development. All students should be encouraged to meet with somebody from Career Services early in their college careers. Since guided internships and other structured work experiences are especially important for students with AS as they consider the transition to work, we suggest early and frequent contact with this office. We deal with this in more detail in Chapter 13.

Important roles within Career Services include career counseling, where the student and the counselor discuss interests, goals, and motivations. This is another opportunity for your student to meet with a knowledgeable adult who may be able to help him craft his special interests (for example, anime) into a concrete plan for a major (computer sciences or film), a plan for an

All students should be encouraged to meet with somebody from Career Services early in their college careers.

internship search, and a viable career goal. Career counselors can also help the student develop their interests and special attributes into a good résumé that will assist in securing placements.

Academic Support Centers

These venues include tutoring centers, language labs, writing labs, and other academic support. Most of these offices offer some degree of content tutoring; that is, subject-specific tutoring. Tutoring may be delivered by peers, graduate students, or professional learning specialists. Remember that these individuals are probably not expert in working with students with disabilities, nor is the college required to provide this sort of tutor.

If your student needs specialized tutoring, talk with Disability Services about the availability of these kinds of services on campus or to get a referral to an off-campus professional in the area.

Many campuses also offer strategy tutoring. This type of tutor can be especially valuable for the student with AS, as most of the work will center on organization, time management, breaking assignments down into manageable pieces, developing long-range project goals, and active reading comprehension – all areas in which students with AS often struggle. On some campuses, the Disability Services office houses strategy tutors, who offer a good way to monitor student progress towards tutoring goals. Many campuses charge a separate fee for this sort of tutoring.

Help your student understand that academic advising is an important resource in his overall college plan and check often that he is using the advisor well.

Academic Advising

Academic advisors may be people who merely sign registration cards, or they can serve as important academic coaches and mentors on campuses. Many are trained as academics, while others (especially freshman advisors) are trained as counselors. In addition to their basic roles, academic advisors can assist in developing students' self-awareness and self-advocacy. The process of advising requires that the student meet with the advisor to discuss her interests, goals, and the reasons she might be interested in choosing a particular major, for example. Advisors have a direct link to professors, and thus can assist students in evaluating their performance in any given class at any given time.

We suggest that your student try to meet with his or her academic advisors at least once per week at the beginning of the semester so that difficulties are identified as soon as possible. Balancing the schedule to account for difficulty of courses, down time, and time to work on/enjoy social activities is of the utmost importance. Help your student understand that academic advising is an important resource in his overall college plan and check often that he is using the advisor well.

In this chapter we presented an overview of some of the offices on campus that you and your student should get to know. The offices within the areas of Student Affairs (especially Disability Services, tutoring, Residence Life, and Mental Health) may be the most important in the beginning, with the offices of Academic Affairs becoming more important once your student settles in. In the next chapter, we will present some strategies for getting your student settled in his new environment.

One of the best tips Alicia's father ever gave her was to read the phone book in order to find out who people are and what they do. She obtained a copy of the campus phone book at her small private college, and with her usual attention to detail, she memorized all of the offices and the names of the people. She wishes she could find out their birthdays and memorize those as well but has settled for learning all of the office locations. When she needed repairs to her leaky bathroom, she looked in the book under "Building and Grounds" and found the phone number of janitorial service. They instructed her on how to file a form for a repair that was needed in her dorm room. When it was time to register for classes for the spring semester, she understood that she had an advisor in her department who could help with course selection. When she is confused she knows to call Disability Services for information and direction. Her parents feel comfortable that they also know the roles of each of the offices on campus due to the close attention they paid during orientation and welcome sessions.

CHAPTER 7

The Incoming Freshman

Andrew and his parents are leaving for freshman orientation. He has not reviewed the materials the college sent him and has no idea of what to expect. His parents have never sent a child to college before and don't know what to expect either. Andrew will spend two nights living in a dormitory with 600 incoming freshmen. He is scared that he will not be able to meet anyone and that he will be too nervous to ask for help if he does not know where to go or what to do. Why do they have to have orientation anyway? And as to what comes next – maybe staying at home was a better idea.

Most of us can remember our own introductions to college life: The buildings that others seemed to move in and out of so casually were unfamiliar, and the physical layout of the campus was confusing. We didn't know the lingo – acronyms such as TF (teaching fellow) or TA (teaching assistant) were meaningless for the first few weeks. Changing sections of a class felt like a monumental task.

In this chapter, we will present specific strategies to use in the weeks leading up to the big start date. We will review some aspects of freshman orientation and how to begin setting up services on campus and other areas that should be worked on early in the semester – namely, getting familiar with the campus layout and operations and learning to ask for help.

How and Where to Start?

The beginning of the academic year is a time of frenetic activity on campus and within the Disability Services office as well. Staff and administrators are focused on new and returning students and dealing with the inevitable crises that crop up. This is hardly the ideal environment in which to successfully begin from scratch with a student on the spectrum. A more successful approach would be to work with the college with a view towards taking care of arrangements prior to the beginning of the semester. We suggest working with the Disability Services office to identify a point person who will be willing (with the student's permission) to have some contact with the family or clinician regarding the student's progress.

We encourage parents to make arrangements for the student to meet with this point person prior to the beginning of the term so that the student can become familiar and comfortable with him/her. This is also an ideal time to establish regular meetings between the student and Disability Services, as it is important for students to meet with someone at least once during the first week of classes, preferably twice, to ensure that he understands how things operate at college and to establish levels of expectation regarding the working relationship between the student and his point person.

Much needs to be accomplished between acceptance to college and the beginning of the school year, and the successful transition to college hinges in part on having a solid action plan in place that has been developed collaboratively by all the stakeholders.

Before Arriving on Campus in the Fall

Before students arrive for their first term at college, we suggest that the student and her parents work with counselors, Disability Services, and other administrators such as the offices planning freshman orientation and the Dean of Students to collaborate on developing materials and strategies aimed at gently transitioning the student into the new and unfamiliar educational institution.

An ideal time to begin this process is during the spring Open House. Every school has an Open House for all admitted students so that undecided students can make a decision about which college to attend, and students who know they want to attend get a second look.

The successful transition to college hinges in part on having a solid action plan in place that has been developed collaboratively by all the stakeholders.

Approach Disability Services staff and others and offer to assist them in developing a process for your son or daughter that they can also apply when working with the inevitable influx of other students with AS who are arriving on college campuses, and let them know that any procedures and products such as handouts, scripts, etc., that are developed for your student are theirs for use with others. At the very least, parents should schedule a meeting with the Disability Services office, as it is as important for parents to get a clear and concrete sense of which specific supports can provided, what will be necessary to initiate these supports, what the student's role will be in accessing the supports, and who will be available to guide and advocate on behalf of the student.

Further, most colleges have a new student orientation over the summer during which incoming students are introduced to their academic advisors, select their first semester courses, obtain their student ID cards, learn about co-curricular activities, and begin the transition process into the institution. This is another great opportunity to get prepared for fall.

Many months before students arrive on campus, we suggest that the student and his parents work with guidance counselors, Disability Services, and other professionals to create guides to the campus, and, if possible, visit campus before orientation begins. Families should prepare to call a number of offices to try to coordinate efforts, understanding that high school and college offices will likely not speak to each other directly. The family must remain the lynch pin of the process, optimally with the student taking a major role.

We have utilized binders with plastic page protectors to create an individualized campus binder for students. Ideally, these guides include the following:

Campus Guide

☐ Map of the campus

☐ Campus addresses, email, phone numbers, and office hours of instructors, teaching assistants, and advisor

☐ Doctors' phone numbers

☐ Yearly, monthly and daily calendar

☐ Space for class schedules and copies of syllabi

☐ Phone numbers of useful staff and administrators (including Disability Services, Health Services, residence hall director, academic advisor, counselor, etc.)

☐ Pharmacy phone number and directions if refills are not available on campus

☐ Shuttle bus routes and schedule if applicable

☐ Student Conduct Code

☐ Dining hall hours of operation

☐ Location of laundry facilities with a "how-to sheet"

☐ Name of barber or hairdresser in the area with phone number and visual map or bus directions

☐ Names and addresses of local restaurants

For colleges situated in more urban environments, parts of the city that are not safe after dark or are generally less safe may be identified. If the college or Disability Service program does not have such a guide, it can be a particularly useful exercise for the student and his parents to create one during a visit to campus. As an active participant in the process of creating a guide, the student can gain a sense of familiarity with the environment that simply reading a guide will not provide.

As an active participant in the process of creating a guide, the student can gain a sense of familiarity with the environment that simply reading a guide will not provide.

Create a Glossary of Terms

Terms such as *teaching assistants, syllabus, on reserve*, and the informal names for buildings such as the Student Center can trip up any student during the first weeks of class. Parents can learn these terms with the student over the summer so that when the student arrives for orientation, she will not be struggling to navigate a new language along with all the other new experiences. These terms can also be added to the student's binder of information.

Review the Campus View/Orientation Booklet

This is a book of pictures and general information about the campus. However, even when available, these booklets typically are not as in-depth as needed.

Study the Student Handbook

The student handbook generally provides more solid information and can be used to build on the information in the orientation booklet. To enable everyone to begin the familiarization process, parents should obtain a copy of each as soon as the student has sent the college a deposit. If a current copy of these materials is not yet available, ask for a copy of the previous year's publications and information about any significant changes such as new buildings, renamed buildings, or change in location of departments the student is likely to frequent (such as the registrar's office, financial aid or bursar's office). Teaming up during summer orientation with a friendly student recommended by one of the support offices on campus is one additional approach to helping the student with AS become familiar with the new school.

Shadow Another Student

In the spring after acceptance, talk to staff at the office of the Dean of Students, student orientation, or Disability Services to arrange for your student to shadow a freshman through an entire day and evening. A demonstration of a "typical day in the life of a student" can give students a sense of what college classes look like and how a day is generally structured. Parents can rendezvous with their student to review what she has been experiencing while the freshman mentor is studying or meeting in a study group. This experience can also give parents insight into additional areas on which to focus over the summer in order to bring their student to readiness for her own entry into college in the fall.

Attend Summer Orientation

Most colleges offer general orientation sessions during the summer for incoming freshman, and a few offer special orientations to freshmen with disabilities. This is different than the shadowing day mentioned above. The orientation is more structured and required of students where the shadow day is optional and set up by the student. For orientation, we suggest a supplemental campus orientation booklet specifically designed for the individual student. A friendly student (often a student worker in the orientation or Disability Services office) can assist the student in preparing his own book. Please see the suggestions below for a list of what to include in this guide/booklet. It is often possible to arrive a few days early or stay a few days later in order to receive more personalized guidance.

A "typical day in the life of a student" can give students a sense of what college classes look like and how a day is generally structured.

It is useful to identify the activities that all students may be involved in during the orientation and compile this information into a guide to orientation for your student with AS. We suggest that, to the extent possible, various speakers on the program, along with the roles they play at the college, be identified to the student in advance. This can be done in conjunction with Disability Services, but is also a great activity for the student and parents to enjoy together in the months leading up to matriculation.

Finally, many schools use peer mentors or orientation leaders as part of the orientation program. If the school does not have an arrangement like this, parents may want to request it. Mentors are typically selected by the disability (support) services center for the purpose of helping the student become better oriented and more comfortable with his new environment.

Create an Area and Campus Guidebook

In much the same ways as attendees at an out-of-town conference receive materials providing concrete information and support about restaurants, shopping, movie theaters, and sites in the area, we suggest compiling a packet of information about the area in which the school is situated. If the school is located in a more remote area, this guide can provide information about how students travel from campus to outside locations such as the closest shopping district or other recreational areas. This information can be incorporated into the student information binder outlined above. In addition, many colleges offer resources on getting to know the area, local restaurants, movie venues, etc., directly on the orientation or college websites.

Take Trial Runs

Trial runs of typical routes on campus that a student will walk can take place during orientation for students who do not live within a reasonable visiting distance from the school. But for families who live within driving distance, doing a more practical tour – or several of them, possibly with campus support staff – is preferable, increasing the student's chance of succeeding in those first few days of class.

Tours can start at the student's dormitory, move to the closest laundry facility and dining halls, and progress to the main classroom buildings in the student's college or department. Other common campus points should be toured, including the after-hours food court, post office, bookstore, health center, student center, and libraries. It may be helpful to time these runs so that the student can schedule when to leave for class, or when to leave the dining hall to get to class. This is also a good time to locate several potential comfortable study spaces. The run-through should be tailored as much as possible to the individual student. Students who will be commuting to campus may be assisted in finding a central point – it could be the Disability Services office, the student center, or a library – where the student goes between classes. Then, the student can practice fanning out the timed runs from that location.

After Arriving on Campus in the Fall

After the student's arrival on campus, support staff usually has no further ongoing contact with parents. However, we have found parental involvement to be essential to success for new students with AS. Different schools have different policies about the level of involvement that is considered appropriate. Don't be reluctant to speak with support staff to determine the campus' policy regarding parental involvement for students on the spectrum. The campus should not hesitate to inform parents when a health or safety issue has arisen but that may be all they are willing to disclose.

After the student's arrival on campus, support staff usually has no further ongoing contact with parents.

Different campuses interpret students' privacy differently, with some campuses more willing to discuss student issues than others. Privacy laws apply to general information provided to (adult) college students; however, health and safety should trump these concerns. If your student will be meeting regularly with a staff member in Disability Services, we suggest you negotiate directly with that individual the amount of contact he or she is comfortable having with you.

Course Selection and Registration

Registration procedures for beginning students differ depending on the size of the campus. Smaller private schools may have in-person registration, while larger public universities may handle all registration online. However, many colleges, regardless of size, have adopted the practice of doing course selection and registration as part of the new student summer orientation schedule of activities.

In some majors such as engineering, the hard sciences, and allied health (nursing or physical therapy, for example), students may have pre-established schedules and, therefore, not have any input or role in course selection for their first term at college. In any event, it is best to be informed and prepared. A call to the department of the student's major can be helpful in determining the name of the advisor and the course selection and registration processes.

Whichever way students register, they usually have access to a school's online course catalog

Be aware, however, that on most campuses, Disability Services staff does not provide registration advising beyond process and procedures.

prior to registration. We suggest that the student and his or her "team" spend some time during the summer perusing the course offerings, requirements, electives, and guidelines for registration. Course selection is not accidental, and students should have some idea of what they wish to register for before they fill out the forms.

In some cases, a freshman advisor is available at orientation to meet with families to determine which courses to consider. In addition, programs with very strong support for students with disabilities provide registration advising. Be aware, however, that on most campuses, Disability Services staff does not provide registration advising beyond process and procedures. In other words, Disability Services will explain the process to students and their families and help the student determine when to meet with an advisor, but they will not register students for classes. Nevertheless, some Disability Services have a "Registration Tips Sheet" that helps students through registration for upcoming terms (see sample below). This might include information about the preregistration and registration process, such as important dates, times, places, and policies, as well as information about how to make changes and corrections and handle situations where the student missed or skipped steps. In some cases, it is as simple as identifying required courses, prerequisites, and dates by which to register.

Sample Registration Planning Sheet: Spring Semester					
Course Name and Number	Pre-requi-sites	Meet With Advisor or Professor?	Register (online or in person)	Date Due	Done
EN102 Freshman English second semester	None		On-line	Nov. 29	Nov. 12
CH201 Chemistry II	Chem I or equiv-alent	Meet with Chem dept about AP Chem		Nov. 29	
MA120 Cal-culus	MA100 or equiv-alent	Not needed	On line	Nov. 29	Nov. 12
SP102 Spanish second semester	SP101	Meet with advisor to discuss if grade of "D" in SP102 will be OK		Nov. 29	
Cardio Kickboxing	None	None	In person	Until class is filled	Nov. 12
Required Courses: (discuss with advisor and fill in here) Foreign Langue: Math: Lab Science English:					

Identifying the registration period in advance and discussing it prior to the actual registration period can smooth the registration experience. Doing so can also help reduce the level of anxiety a student (or her parents) experience when deadlines are missed or steps are forgotten.

In this chapter we talked about how to get your student off to a good start by visiting campus multiple times, creating a guide and arranging a mentor through Disability Services. In the next chapter, we continue this theme with an insider's look at how you can best collaborate with Disability Services to foster your student's success.

Eric has almost completed his first quarter at college, and for the most part he is liking it so far. He has made a few friends that he hangs out with and goes to the animé club meetings with. One of his friends asked him yesterday if he had registered for next quarter yet, as he had gotten an email instructing him to do so at 6:30 a.m. that day. Eric had told himself he'd go online after the club meeting but had forgotten, and now it is the weekend. When he went on the college's website to choose classes, it prohibited Eric from registering, instead stating that there was a "HOLD" on his record and that he should consult his advisor for an explanation. Eric was confused and frustrated. What was a "hold," and why was it there? He'd never met with anybody called an advisor, and how was he to find out who this person was anyway? Eric told himself he'd deal with it next week, and emailed his online friends instead.

Eric would have been much better prepared to register for classes if he had better control of his schedule and managed his time. His agenda should have noted to identify and meet with his advisor at least two weeks before registration. The advisor could have removed the holds so he could register.

CHAPTER 8

Working With Disability Services

Alicia has called home crying four times this week. She got into a different English class than she wanted, and they have to read all these books with real people in them. She just can't write the paper that is due on Friday. The professor seems to expect her to know how the girl in To Kill a Mockingbird *would describe her father. How could she know that, and how can she write three pages about it? There must be a way for her not to have to take these kinds of classes; there must be a law!*

When her parents called Disability Services, they were told they would work with Alicia and her professor to determine reasonable accommodations but pointed out that she would not be exempt from the writing assignments.

Families transitioning to college learn about new levels of service and new offices, as discussed previously. One of the most important offices in the life of your child at college, whether he or she received special education in high school or not, is the office of Disability Services. Many families fear this relationship will be contentious, a fear we hope we have dispelled in Chapter 5 by presenting the changes in your student's legal status and underscoring his or her status as a student with a disability.

In this chapter, we will introduce you to the workings and philosophy of these offices and provide an insider's view of how families can best develop the team approach necessary for your student's continued success.

What Is Disability Services?

On most campuses, the office of Disability Services variably named Disability Resource Center, Access Services, Student Disability Services, etc., is the authorizing body for students with disabilities. In other words, students must be cleared through this office to be recognized as "students with disabilities" for the purposes of receiving services and accommodations. Disability Services should be contacted as soon as a student is accepted and knows he will attend a particular college.

Numerous lawsuits have turned on whether the student had properly self-identified to the appropriate body on campus. Failure to do so jeopardizes students' exercise of their legal rights under the ADA and Section 504. All colleges in the United States are required to have a designated agent on campus that is responsible for students with disabilities.

Smaller colleges may have a professor or dean under whom these duties fall. Such persons may not be particularly expert in different disability types and may only know the basics of disability compliance. Such colleges, therefore, may need more education from the student and/or the family in order to ensure the student's needs are met.

Larger colleges and universities typically have free-standing offices that are professionally staffed by disability experts. Encourage your student to get to know the staff, to be a frequent visitor, to use the office as a resource when he or she does not know where else to turn. Disability Services professionals usually know everyone on campus and are quite comfortable in the role of resource locator.

Disability Services should be contacted as soon as a student is accepted and knows he will attend a particular college.

Are Disability Services AS Experts?

Disability Services offices are typically staffed by professional disability experts who may work with students with physical and medical, sensory, learning, cognitive, psychiatric, and other disabilities. Few providers would consider themselves experts at working with students with AS, but in recent years, more and more have sought special training in this area. Still, you and your student want to be prepared to inquire, educate (when necessary), and fully disclose to the appropriate provider.

While smaller colleges with one designated disability contact may be excellent choices for the student with AS, the depth of understanding of the particulars of these disorders may or may not be a strength of the one- or two-person office. Larger colleges and universities may have support staff with expertise in working with students with psychiatric disabilities, learning disabilities, or attention disorders, who may also have experience with AS. Many practitioners have personal experience with children or have friends or relatives on the spectrum.

A small but growing number of colleges and universities are developing specialized AS support programs with trained staff. For these reasons, we implore you to inquire specifically whether the disability staff is experienced with AS students as soon as the student is accepted to the school or, preferably, when the student is looking at colleges (see Chapter 1). Many families and professionals view Disability Services as a barrier to accommodations and services and, indeed, the more stringent processes of higher education may give that impression. However, Disability Services can serve as the main resource for qualified students with AS on campuses.

What Does Disability Services Do?

Disability Services professionals evaluate documentation for a range of conditions, including AS. They are also charged with understanding the academic requirements and standards of their individual colleges, as well as the relevant state, local, and federal disability and higher education laws. They also must understand the wider culture of their college, including residence life, student activities, etc. Thus, they are tasked with not only providing students with accommodations but also with protecting the interests of the college or university at which they work.

For students with AS, the office of Disability Services can play a number of roles. On some campuses, the office plays a very narrow role, limited to policy for students with disabilities, review of documentation, negotiating accommodations, and acting as a resource for students, faculty, and staff. On other campuses, Disability Services providers take on an expanded role, which can include providing mentoring and special services for the student with AS. In addition, some offices provide mentors for socializing, social skills groups or teaching, specialized sections of the first-year seminar, and so on. Direct, but respectful inquiries should give you a clear picture of the philosophy and working practices of the Disability Services office at your college of choice. Please refer to the checklist of questions to ask in Chapter 2.

Disability Services providers can authorize accommodations in class, negotiate special housing requests, and work with students to understand their rights and responsibilities. In a broader role, this office can also educate faculty, administration, and staff about students with AS and mediate any misunderstandings that arise. Further, a Disability Services expert

Direct, but respectful inquiries should give you a clear picture of the philosophy and working practices of the Disability Services office at your college of choice.

may act as the point person for crisis management and a source of professional information and referrals, and the Disability Services office can become a "safe space" for the student. Most are also dedicated advocates for people with disabilities. Even if your student does not seek accommodations, don't make the mistake of thinking your student can do it alone without involving this office.

Will Disability Services Disclose the Diagnosis?

As discussed, Disability Services will not disclose a diagnosis for the student; indeed, they are prohibited by law from doing so. Similarly, most offices will not negotiate accommodations or adjustments for a student. Rather, staff will work with the student so that he may develop self-advocacy skills. Understanding that many students with AS lack the social acumen to be good self-advocates, disability providers often work more intensively with such students so that they can achieve the highest level of self-determination possible.

Will Disability Services Evaluate Students?

Some Disability Services offices include testing centers in which assessment of students is conducted. Many of these offices are within the structure that includes counseling, rather than within Student Affairs or centers where research is being conducted. However, assessment is not within the purview of most Disability Services offices, but they are usually prepared to refer students to experts on or off campus (depending on the resources in the region). Many offices keep lists of lower-fee assessment clinics, providers who are experienced in AS, therapists, psychiatrists, and tutors.

Partnering Between Disability Services and Families

In our experience, partnering with Disability Services in the early stage of the transition process is important. The first stage may begin with a call from you to the Disability Services office before the campus visit, followed by a meeting with the student and family (perhaps when you tour the campus or come for an interview). When you provide information and documentation to the Disability Services staff, including relevant information about personal habits, soothing strategies, response to stress, changes in family dynamics, and so on, you set your son or daughter up for success. Withholding important information (like the fact that an aide was provided right up until high school graduation) is a recipe for disaster.

Be prepared to hear that students are now adults and that you cannot participate in the process. This is a legal interpretation of the law and philosophy on many campuses. When you discuss directly with the Disability Services office that you would like to be a partner in the transition and respect their professional role and knowledge, you are well on your way to forging a good relationship. We feel strongly that successful transition to higher education for students on the spectrum requires ongoing communication between the student, Disability Services, and the parents.

The following table lists examples of typical accommodations requested by students with AS. Those in the left-hand column may have been possible and supported in the high school environment but will most likely be considered "unreasonable" in college settings. The accommodations in the right-hand column, on the other hand, are generally considered "reasonable" in postsecondary education.

"Unreasonable" Accommodations – Typical in High School	Reasonable Accommodations – Typical in College Settings
Acceptance of behavior that disrupts classroom	Brief breaks to step outside class
Provision of copies of materials when student is not present in class	Notetaker to provide additional copies of classroom notes (student with AS must still take own also)
Unlimited time or test divided into multiple parts	Up to double time extension to take tests
Highlighted texts or study guides	Brief, individual clarification with instructor
Waiver from group work	Assistance identifying designated role in group
Retake of tests	None
Aide or paraprofessional	None
Scribe or reader	Assistive software

In this chapter we provided some insiders' tips on working with Disability Services. In the next chapter, we will discuss specific academic issues and difficulties some students on the spectrum encounter and discuss accommodations that may be of help.

Andrew needed extra time for a math test. He went to Disability Services and was very upset. He had forgotten to talk to his professor about the accommodation, and the test was that day. He needed the extra time, or he would flunk. He just knew it. Why did he think he could be a college student anyway!

The person at the desk saw that Andrew was very upset. He interrupted the Disability Services person Andrew usually worked with and asked her to talk to Andrew. The Disability Services person told Andrew she would make a call and talk to the professor with Andrew right after the appointment she was currently in the middle of. She got Andrew some water and directed him to an office where he could calm down and wait for her. She also told Andrew that he had done the right thing by coming to her office and trying to figure this out with assistance. Finally, she also cautioned him that when the issue of this test was resolved, he would need to work out a better way to remember to set up his extended time testing accommodations at the beginning of each semester because professors are entitled to request timely notice of the accommodation students are requesting. In addition, making sure his accommodation is in place can help Andrew prevent this level of anxiety prior to a potentially stressful event such as a test.

CHAPTER 9

Academic Issues Your Student May Encounter

Molly thinks she may want to major in business, but she heard that the business school at her university uses a team model in which work groups do large projects, which are then presented to the entire class. She is nervous as she does not like to work in groups. When she gets anxious, she can't speak up. She is deathly afraid of talking in front of more than one or two others. She also finds that the other students don't always work up to her level. Maybe she will choose an English major instead.

In this chapter we will move to issues of academic rigor and complexity that your son or daughter will no doubt face in the higher education environment. We will seek to clarify and to prepare you for some of the differences in accommodation availability and make recommendations for preparing for the inevitable changes as early as possible.

What Are Academic Accommodations?

As discussed in Chapter 5, accommodations under the ADA are defined as adjustments to an academic program or environment intended to mitigate the impact of the functional limitations of a disability on participation in that environment. Adjusting academic assignments, changing classrooms to enable physical access, and alternate-format books (audio or computer disks

129

rather than print) are all examples of accommodations commonly provided on college campuses. Known for "leveling the playing field," accommodations make the academic environment manageable without fundamentally altering the curriculum.

Students and parents are often frustrated to find that accommodations they used in high school are not provided by their student's college. Many modifications like unlimited time for exams, exams interpreted for the student, reduced reading assignments, etc. would be construed as providing an unfair advantage over other equally qualified students and in most cases, would not be authorized. Please keep in mind that the postsecondary system is governed by laws that guarantee *equal access* rather than success (see Chapter 5). This is a seismic change in philosophy that is difficult for many families to grasp.

Adjusting academic assignments, changing classrooms to enable physical access, and alternate-format books (audio or computer disks rather than print) are all examples of accommodations commonly provided on college campuses.

Here we will briefly review some needs and associated academic adjustments. Every student with AS is different; therefore, it is impossible to offer a complete list of reasonable and unreasonable accommodations. Instead, we will discuss a few domains, the importance of which parents and clinical teams may not be aware.

Writing

Many students with AS struggle with writing tasks related to problems in executive functioning (planning, organizing, procrastinating, etc.), as well as problems with integration and synthesis. Sometimes the difficulty lies in having to take the perspective of characters in an assigned reading or understanding the professor's perspective in the assignment. Nevertheless, all students must write in college, and most colleges have a required writing curriculum.

Many students benefit from using dictation software or webbing programs. Especially for those who find the initial act of committing pencil to paper daunting, sometimes being able to talk through the paper out loud, move around while dictating, or draw their ideas – which speech-to-text and mapping software allows – helps students move past the initial road block that the writing process presents them.

Other students benefit from the assistance of a writing tutor or coach. Please don't be that parent who edits assignments that are sent home each week – this is a slippery slope to academic misconduct for your student. Any assistance at the college level that even can be remotely misconstrued as work being done by someone other than the student may be considered plagiarism or academic dishonesty.

Faculty might consider leniency in grading of assignments in light of the fundamental requirements of their courses when asked to make accommodations, such as allowing the student to tie a topic of special interest into a writing assignment, but formal accommodations for writing assignments would be best discussed with the Disability Services staff.

Test Taking

Taking tests may not be a problem for your student. Memorizing information and repeating it back may be a strength and a skill in which he (and you) take pride. However, some students do struggle with exams, and benefit from accommodation such as distraction reduction, no scantrons (bubble sheets), or extra time.

Individual exam accommodation needs are determined by the Disability Services staff and communicated to students and faculty in various ways, depending on the campus. On some campuses, a letter is delivered to the professor by the student. Other campuses use an email notification. In most circumstances, it is the student's responsibility to deliver the accommodation letter.

Some campuses have testing centers within the office of Disability Services, while others require students to work directly with their professors to make exam arrangements.

It is important to find out which model a campus uses and to be sure the student is prepared for the eventuality of exams. All students could use training in how to study for exams in college, as discussed in the following pages, and the authors highly recommend that students seek out and utilize academic or study skills support offices on campus for guidance.

Taking Notes

Many students with AS take copious and detailed notes but have problems separating out the important information. Other students pride themselves on their capacity to recall everything they read or hear and prefer not to take notes. Still others would like to take notes but cannot write fast enough, become too distracted, panic in crowded classrooms, or cannot remember well. For these reasons, many students with AS benefit from note takers in classes.

Individual campuses handle note taking differently, from handing out special carbon-copied paper to asking other students to be note takers to enlisting peers who are paid to provide typed or handwritten copies of their notes. These systems are arranged by Disability Services.

It is important to investigate in advance the individual school's note-taking policies and requirements to make sure the documentation supports note takers also and to discuss with your student his or her need for this essentially non-stigmatizing support. New technology includes "smart pens" that record lectures as students write on special paper and replay a section of the lecture when the relevant note is touched (www.livescribe.com).

Many students with AS take copious and detailed notes but have problems separating out the important information.

Alternate but effective accommodations include audio-taping lectures or using a laptop for note taking. Do not assume that these are automatically allowed in classrooms; faculty can and do forbid laptops during their lectures. Many others object to being audio taped. Follow the guidance of the Disability Services office at your campus to be sure that these requests are handled correctly.

Studying and Integrating New Information

Because students with AS tend to see only one perspective (i.e., cannot see the forest for the trees), they often miss the connections that make up the whole. This can be a problem on exams, papers, projects, and other activities.

Prior to coming to campus, we encourage parents to begin to work with their student and their educational and clinical teams to understand any deficits in integration and how they might impact the student so that appropriate accommodations and support can be sought. For example, there may be review books that summarize course information to supplement assigned readings.

Alternately, many professors are happy to assist students with learning how to draw inferences from the readings and combine that with lecture materials so as to be more successful in the class. All instructors are required to have office hours set aside for just such assistance. Students are well advised to use their syllabi to find out each instructor's hours and to visit during these times.

Because students with AS tend to see only one perspective (i.e., cannot see the forest for the trees), they often miss the connections that make up the whole.

Some students require the services of a professional tutor in order to achieve this level of understanding. This is unlikely to be provided free of charge or as an accommodation. Students may have to ask their instructors or department chairperson to identify potential upper-classmen who excel in the particular academic area and who may charge for their assistance by the hour.

Reading

Students with AS are often characterized as early and strong readers. However, many struggle with advanced reading comprehension. This is because of the problems discussed with regard to integration and synthesis. That is, a student may well understand the words she reads but not be able to form a cohesive picture of how all the details and individual sections add up to one greater lesson. As above, the difficulty may lie in understanding the motivation and emotions of characters in fiction.

Utilizing audio books (now commercially available in many formats) and training in active reading strategies are promising tools for students with AS who struggle to focus and understand their reading. Students are advised to check with the Disability Services office at their institution for information on the process and availability of such assistance.

Organization and Planning

If the student has problems with organization and planning, you are no stranger to the concept of "executive functioning" and know the tremendous impact this has on many aspects of your student's life. From keeping track of the day's schedule of classes and appointments to organizing the study area and tools needed to complete an assignment, these are all aspects necessary to a student's daily success and management of the college environment.

Students with AS may get overwhelmed and frustrated, or insist that they do not need to use organizational or time management strategies to stay on top of their work. Indeed, their intellectual gifts and excellent memory have enabled some students with AS to manage well; however, many arrive on campus with underdeveloped skills in multi-tasking, juggling studying with outside assignments, or managing several long-range projects at the same time. Some students cannot complete their work until is perfect; others cannot even get projects started. Few come with good time management tools beyond a cell phone (if that).

As discussed in Chapters 1 and 2, please do your student a favor and make sure she has been trained to use planners, agendas, to-do lists, white boards, sticky notes, and the like, prior to applying to college. At the very latest, start in the summer prior to senior year with a daily chores chart at home listing re-occurring activities like wake-up, bedtime, and even meal times. The student can then practice adding single-occurrence activities, special events, etc. Continued use of such a chart pays off later on.

We know that students are reluctant and often see no need to use such simplistic tools, especially when they view their schedules as exceedingly static and predictable. However, once at college, each day inevitably brings a different class schedule. If using some type of planner is not familiar prior to starting college, it is highly unlikely that a student with AS will "pick up" on how to use one without assistance and monitoring after college has begun, when so many other new demands are urgent.

Students with AS may get overwhelmed and frustrated, or insist that they do not need to use organizational or time management strategies to stay on top of their work.

Working in Groups

Many college classes and programs emphasize (indeed, many require) group work in labs, in projects, on teams, and the like. For example, no one gets through an engineering or business program these days without extensive teamwork. Many college students with AS have weak social interaction skills. Thus, situations like groups that involve interpersonal interaction are often anxiety producing for them. Other students struggle with having to be perfect and do not feel that others in the group are up to their standards and, therefore, are not good team players.

Working with a group requires interaction, progress checks, renegotiating based on time and assignments, and so on. All of these tasks are socially oriented and present problems for most students with AS. For all the above reasons, much academic group work may require accommodations in order for the student with AS to be successful. Asking for assistance from Disability Services or from faculty in facilitating negotiations with peers is a reasonable request for a student who struggles in this area. However, expecting group activities to be waived is not very realistic.

Making Oral Presentations

Social anxiety, common in students with AS, can interfere with presentations in front of groups. Some students struggle in this area due to the demand for organization and thinking on one's feet. Others struggle because they do not read the social cues of their audience and cannot adjust their presentation accordingly. Whatever the reason for weak presentation skills and related anxiety, various accommodations might be feasible for the student.

Videotaped presentations or presentations to a smaller section of the class might be an option. If not, we suggest that the student over-prepare the presentation with the use of slides, script outlines, etc. We suggest that you work with your student on discussing these issues directly with faculty, if possible, and, certainly with Disability Services. We have worked successfully with many students with these issues and have seen firsthand that it is possible for students to improve their ability to read the social cues of others as well as become more comfortable in their presentation skills.

Alicia is taking an astronomy course and really enjoys it. She loves studying the stars and can and does practically answer every question the professor asks. She is sure her participation grade in the course is good. In fact, she has almost read the whole textbook, and it is only mid-October. She is surprised her classmates aren't as excited about the topic as she is, In fact, many of them slump in their chairs or put their heads down, even when she is elaborating on a reading that she has done the night before. To Alicia, it sometimes feels like she is the only student in the class. After the last class, on the way out the door a classmate abruptly turned and said to her, "Why don't YOU teach the class?" Alicia was perplexed by this, and became even more perplexed when she received a letter the following week from the Dean of Students requesting that she make an appointment to discuss her disruptions in astronomy class.

Interrupting or Disrupting Class

Students with AS are often experts in their areas of interest, but most professors are at a loss about how to deal with a student who rudely calls out corrections in class because she cannot tolerate even minor misstatements or errors on the part of the professor.

It is important to help such a student understand that this type of behavior cannot be tolerated in a classroom, along with eating or drinking, interruptions, leaving the room, or otherwise disrupting the ongoing lesson. Faculty may not be flexible in dealing with such behavior, and it is a situation in which the expertise of the office of Disability Services should be sought.

Parents will want to address any possible behavior issue their student has with the student's disability provider well before it becomes a problem in a class. Students need to learn appropriate behavior control in class, but campuses can also try to understand that sometimes what appears to be rude behavior has an underlying cause (such as an extreme sensory reaction). If yours is a student who had these issues in high school, don't leave it unaddressed when he goes to college.

Student Rights and Responsibilities

We conclude this chapter by a brief statement reminding you that your student has rights, but with those rights come responsibilities. It is your role to make sure that he is up to the responsibility.

Gradually increasing responsibilities in the years before a student goes to college is the best way to ensure that your son or daughter will be ready when the time arrives.

We have discussed academic accommodations in college and what your student may need to learn in order to be prepared for this transition. In the next chapter, we will discuss housing and residential life – perhaps the area where many of our students need the most support. We will discuss different housing options you may consider, such as a single room versus one with a roommate. We will discuss residence hall staffing, disclosure, and handling common roommate issues.

Eric is taking a chemistry class. He enjoyed chemistry in high school, but he is nervous that, like in high school, the teacher will tell students to find their own lab partners and that he would be left out. He was surprised when the person in Disability Services asked him about his prior experiences with group projects. When he told them about all the times he was left out, the staff suggested that he write a note to the professor asking for a meeting to discuss possible accommodations. The professor was happy to assign groups in advance rather than leave it up to chance, thereby reducing further anxiety.

CHAPTER 10
Housing and Residential Life

It was Thursday night and Molly had a 20-page pa-per to work on that was due the following Monday. She did not like working in the library. People she did not know might talk to her or sit at the table where she spread out her research, and that made her uncomfortable and unable to write. Molly preferred to work in her room. She had a single, and it was set up exactly the way she needed to study and write.

As Molly got settled in to begin her paper, the music start-ed – it was loud, and so were the other people on her floor. Molly went into the hall and asked them to quiet down and turn down the music. Several students responded with, "Oh come on, it's Spring Weekend!!" Molly did not know what to do.

Many students and parents are not fully aware of the issues that living on campus may bring up for a student with AS. The intent of this chapter is to illuminate this portion of the college experience so that you and your student can evaluate whether this is a viable option or not. We train residence life staff all across the country, and are confident that if your student is up to the task, the experience can be a great one.

Elements of Communal Living

The most exciting but also one of the most difficult aspects of going off to college may well be the residential piece. Many students with AS want to live on campus in order to "fully experience" college. Their parents (aka you) approach this rite of passage with tremendous anxiety and worry. And you are right to worry, because this part of their education is overwhelming for many students on the spectrum.

Our intent here is not to frighten you but to stimulate you to think about the various aspects of residential life and how your student will be able to cope with them. This realistic appraisal will allow (a) serious decisions about whether the student is ready for living away; and (b) if the answer is "yes," what sort of residential situation would be best and how you and the college can best prepare.

Can you imagine your son or daughter living with a roommate (or three), sharing a bathroom with a wide range of people (maybe even of the opposite sex), dealing with noise, partying, drugs and sex? Does he lack the sophistication and executive functioning required to succeed in the residence halls? Will stress and sensory issues make the residence halls an unwelcoming living space for the student? Will the possibility of having a messy room derail the student's concentration?

If some of these questions make you or your student uneasy, you may have to think twice about your student's preparedness to live away from home. There are quieter floors and quieter dorms, but there is no such thing as a stress-free residence hall on any campus known to us.

Living in a residence hall can be an experience akin to moving to another country – everything is different, where you sleep, when you sleep, what you eat, the shower and the bathroom you use. Also, while there are no "dorm mothers" any more, there are rules that bring sense to communal living. Prepare yourself and your student, for the rules are different from living at home! For example, at home bedtime might have been 10 p.m., now it is often 2 a.m. or later.

The most exciting but also one of the most difficult aspects of going off to college may well be the residential piece.

Students are given a brief orientation to residence life in the first few days; however, this is mostly concerned with the rules and sanctions for drinking, noise, guest policies, how to sign into the building, how to get something fixed, and how to report a problem. Other topics of these orientations generally serve housekeeping functions such as (a) to read the riot act on behavior to the new hall residents; (b) to introduce floor mates, residence hall staff, and other residents of the building; and (c) as a first opportunity for social programming by the residence hall staff.

Unfortunately, the purposes of these meetings and the rules enforced by the residence hall director or residence assistant may not be entirely clear to students on the spectrum. Make sure your student understands that these meetings are important, and most often compulsory. Encourage your student to attend all meetings that are important or mandatory. Sometimes crucial information is disseminated, such as what to do in an emergency, etc.

Who Staffs a Residence Hall?
Residence halls are managed and operated by several types and levels of staff.

Residence Directors (RD)

The RD, at a professional-level position, is in charge of a building or a group of buildings. Most RDs live on campus. They report to an area director on larger campuses or directly to the Dean of Students. RDs manage the residence halls and supervise the residence assistants, who live on the various floors in the dorm.

Encourage your student to attend all meetings that are important or mandatory.

The RD on your student's campus may not have direct contract with your student; however, we believe it is vital that he or she be informed of the student with AS in residence so that the RD can provide extra guidance to the appropriate residence assistants should an issue arise. As soon as your student is assigned to a residence hall, you can inform the RD (ideally, your student will) of your student's AS and possible issues related to residential life. (More on disclosure later in this chapter.)

Residence Assistants (RA/CA)

Residence halls have many levels of professionals and students working on site. Upper-classmen, usually known as residence assistants (RAs) or community assistants (CAs), often live on each floor and are the first reference for students. On some campuses, there may not be RAs in each building as they cover several floors or even several buildings.

We recommend that RAs be informed if a student on the spectrum is living on their floor; however, due to FERPA (The Federal Educational Right and Privacy Act), even if you have already contacted Disability Services and other units at the university, there has been no automatic disclosure of your student's status. That means your student and you have to decide whether to disclose, how much, and to whom.

When RAs are informed, they can assist the student in her transition, roommate issues, practical matters, and any teasing or bullying that may take place. Also, when working with housing on dorm assignment, we suggest that you make it clear that you are looking for a building or residence hall with a strong RA presence.

An excellent way to assist the student in the transition to residence hall living would be to tour the facilities with the student and to introduce him to the RA of the floor and the RD for the building. Summer is a perfect time to do this if the building is open; otherwise, arranging a tour thorough the office of Residential Life may be necessary.

Your college may have a special pre-orientation program that brings students on campus for community service or some other first-year activity during the weeks before classes begin. This is a great time to move the student on the spectrum into his room early to adjust to his new living space and meet/work with staff in smaller groups. Some campuses allow this type of early move-in but others do not. Check with the Residential Life office and with Disability Services for specifics. This would also be a good chance (with your student's permission!) to alert the RD and the RA if the student will need some support in initial involvement in floor activities or meetings.

Disclosure

Disclosure is especially useful if the student is not likely to participate in programmed residence hall activities. Residence staff generally will try to integrate all students in the group, although this may not be the sort of therapeutic intervention you hoped the school would be able to provide. RAs can make suggestions for appropriate activities if a student appears to be having difficulty participating. Perhaps the problem is one of time management, perhaps it is a scheduling problem, or perhaps the events in the residence hall are too visually or auditorily busy and, therefore, overwhelming for the student.

RAs can be the first line of assistance in facilitating social interactions without needing to disclose to the other students the nature of the disability. For example, if the students on a floor are getting together for something social (a movie, ice cream party, etc.), the RA may initially choose a quieter movie activity to try to engage the student with AS. He or she could ask the student to help select a movie or bring the student to the lounge (or movie space) early before the room is full and noisy. The RA may also try to engage the student with AS in an activity with fewer participants.

We believe the benefits of disclosing to RD and RAs outweigh the potential drawbacks

What If You Don't Want to Disclose?

Many students (and their parents) feel that disclosure to residence staff is unnecessary or are reluctant to disclose for fear that it will be stigmatizing. These families may have been coached by guidance counselors, therapists, doctors, or relatives not to reveal too much about their student's status, or the student may not want to be seen as different in his new environment.

We believe the benefits of disclosing to RDs and/or RAs outweigh the potential drawbacks; however, the decision is one that, ultimately, each family must make. Recall that in most instances the school will not be able to make this disclosure on your behalf. If your student is the reluctant one, you as the parent may need to include disclosure to the rules under which you are willing to allow him to live in a residence hall. This again is your family's decision.

Roommates

Living with a roommate is difficult and downright impossible for many students. Roommate issues may be compounded for students with AS, who may lack negotiation and interpersonal interaction skills required to be a successful roommate. Sometimes it is the sharing of small space that is the problem, including the possibility that someone will move or handle the student's stuff. At other times, it is the student with AS who causes problems by not understanding the roommate's boundaries, for example.

The first contact most students have with their new roommates used to be a trepidation-filled phone call. Now students connect via social networking sites such as FaceBook almost as soon as the roommate selection process has been completed. (This differs from school to school; some early summer, some during orientation, some much later, just before classes start.)

Students quickly find their roommates' profile, what songs they like, how they dress, etc. This sort of social savvy comes naturally to typical kids but may not be the case for students with AS. It is not feasible for parents to intervene here beyond suggesting that the student explore this means of finding their roommates and becoming prepared to meet them.

Once students move into their shared rooms, they face choosing a bed, a side of the room, a desk, top bunk or bottom, etc. We strongly suggest that you accompany your student on the first day, if at all possible. Don't feel you need to decorate, but you can be there to assist should the student need it. Did the roommate take all of the best furniture? Did your student have any say in the arrangement of the room? Resolving such issues can be a lesson to both roommates that they are going to have to start negotiating with each other right from the start.

It may take the student with AS extra time to adjust to sharing space and (often) belongings. This may be compounded if the student has sensory sensitivities or rigid routines for keeping his belongings or space organized. Alternately, many students with AS have not learned how to keep their belongings organized and may pose a burden to their roommate.

It may take the student with AS extra time to adjust to sharing space and (often) belongings.

Many of these issues are the same for students who do not have AS; however, the resolution of the conflict may require some additional effort on the part of residence hall staff when a student with AS is involved. Unless the student has been away to camp or school (and many with AS have not!), getting used to a shared bathroom takes time, too. Often sharing a bathroom with other people in the dorm is similar to a camp experience. As one student we work with said, "You said this is now my home, but at home I don't shower with other people in the same room or use a toilet with someone two feet away with a metal wall between us!" To allow time to adjust to the environment, get used to the sounds and smells, set up new routines, etc., is another reason why it may be important for your student to move in early. If assistance is needed with roommate issues, it is important to get help before the situation escalates!

Luke was in his room with the door open playing a video game. Some of the guys from his floor walked by, saw him, and thought the game looked cool. They asked if they could try the game. Luke hates the idea of other people playing his games or using his computer. He had several bad experiences in high school with guys taking his Gameboy and ruining it or kicking him off a computer when he was playing a game. Luke did not want these guys from his residence hall touching his stuff. He yelled at them to get out of his room and started to cry. The other boys laughed and ran away.

A Word About Roommate Contracts

Most schools have roommates fill out a contract that specifies the "rules" of the room. What is the general feeling about guests? Bedtime and lights out? Noise? Smoking? Parties? Signals that privacy is needed?

Often roommates are given a form upon first meeting and told to go off and negotiate. This will likely not favor the student with AS. He may be dominated by a more socially savvy peer or, conversely, might try to dominate the contract through rigid insistence that things be arranged solely according to his preferences.

We suggest that the help of the RA be sought if it appears that negotiating the very first contract will be problematic. RAs have been trained to do this discreetly and do not have to reveal to the new roommate that the student has social difficulties.

Cleanliness, Order, and Rigidity

Adhering to rigid order and cleanliness is the way some students with AS understand their world. For these students, it is inconceivable that belongings are out of place or the room is a mess. As this is not the way many college students live, there is a strong disconnect between the student with AS and other students and possible roommates in that respect.

We know from raising them that students with AS use rigidity as a means to control their environment; that is, it allows them to better understand and structure their everyday activities. Some students insist that their room in the residence hall mirror their room at home.

Since most students with AS are extremely visual, creating a space that visually replicates the home environment might be the student's goal. It is a great idea (if possible) to recreate *some* aspects of the familiar surroundings, such as which side of the room, lighting conditions, familiar bedspread and pillows, pictures or maps from home, etc. Precious belongings or special collections (especially if they are valuable or weapons-related) must be left at home!

Is a Single Room the Best Solution?

We know from raising them that students with AS use rigidity as a means to control their environment; that is, it allows them to better understand and structure their everyday activities.

Many parents and RDs believe that the best way to avoid roommate conflicts is to assign the student with AS to a single room. But wait! While this is often a great solution, it is not always necessary. Sometimes having a single from the start isolates the student from the mainstream of dormitory life. We have known students who never left their single rooms except to go to class and meals. We know one who showered in the middle of the night so he would not encounter any floor mates.

On some campuses, single rooms are found in the typical freshman residence halls, but on many campuses singles exist only in smaller or in specialty houses that are full of upper-classmen (juniors and seniors). This would further isolate a younger student with AS from his or her age peers.

When a student is very rigid, has never shared space, has sensory sensitivities that would be aggravated by the presence of a roommate, or needs substantial down time away from others, we lean towards recommending a single. If a student has had an unsuccessful roommate pairing at another school or in another hall, we also favor a single. Often the best possible solution is a single room in a suite in which the student has her own space but shares the bathrooms and has suite mates with whom to interact. Nevertheless, one of us monitored a student who went an entire semester without ever meeting his suite mates!

Who to Talk to About Getting a Single Room

If you have decided with your student and the support team that a single room is the best option, we suggest you discuss this with the Disability Services office at your college of choice. This office will be able to provide guidance with regard to policy and procedures for requesting a single room as an accommodation and the sort of medical documentation you would need. On some campuses, Disability Services handles housing accommodations, but on others it is done by Housing. Find out and start early, because it is often possible to tour the various types of singles and have direct input into the process. This is not very likely during peak times such as the month before school starts.

Parties

Parties are a fact of life on most campuses in the country. Many parties take place in the residence hall, hence a discussion is included in this section. Students need to understand that parties will occur around them, possibly even in their own room. Because students with AS may not understand or enjoy the social nature of residence halls, the noise and partying can be disruptive and overwhelming to them.

Optimally, setting guidelines for noisy parties should be part of the roommate contract, and if that is not respected, the assistance of the RA or RD may be necessary. To circumvent this problem, many students and their families opt for an honors dorm, specialty house, wellness or substance-free dorm (no alcohol, no drugs), or a dorm with enforced quiet hours if these choices are available.

Students should understand that when parties involve under-age drinking or drug use, attendance without even partaking carries a substantial risk of judicial sanction. No student wants to "squeal" on their peers, but the student must understand that even if he does not feel comfortable going to an RA, he must leave the room when a party with illegal behavior is going on. Luckily, our rule-bound kids usually do not have any problem with this.

Many students on the spectrum have food preferences that make it difficult for them to eat the food available in the residence halls.

Food and Dietary Issues

Most larger residence halls have dining halls that offer a broader (and palatable) selection of food options. Students quickly find out which dining hall is the best, which has their favorite foods, which include late-night options, etc. Nevertheless many students on the spectrum have food preferences that make it difficult for them to eat the food available in the residence halls.

We suggest that the expertise of the Disability Services office be brought into this conversation, as they may be aware of dieticians and other resources on campus that can help a student with food preferences (or even food allergies) find the best and most tasty options. Seeking the assistance of the Disability Services office in engaging the student in a conversation about dining hall choices can have the added benefit of getting a reticent student to open up about other issues as well, such as hygiene, anxiety over making friends, and academic concerns.

While this is best discussed prior to a student's arrival on campus, at schools that provide this type of flexibility in dining halls, it may not be difficult to provide options consistent with the dietary preferences and needs of a student on the spectrum. If there is no resolution available, some students request to live in an apartment-style residence hall where they have their own kitchen.

Student Safety

A conversation about safety begins at home and should be continued by residence hall staff in orientation. For example, this may be the first time (depending on where they grew up) that students have had to lock doors (interior room doors as well as exterior hall doors).

You might explain to your student before he leaves for college that locking his room is like locking a house in a city there are many people around and you don't know everyone. We don't want to frighten students, but unlocked doors in residence halls invite theft of valuable property such as laptops, phones, and mp3 players. Safety and/or locks for laptops may also need to be explained.

Letting strangers into locked residence halls, propping open fire doors, talking to strangers, and attending parties in houses where they don't know anybody are risks that all undergraduates must be cautioned against. This message will be reinforced by residence staff, but the safety talk should not come as a total surprise to your student when it occurs. Remember that our kids are reassured by familiar messages and distressed by new information. Also, many of our students with AS are gullible and trusting, making them easy targets for teasing and jokes.

Further, a frank discussion about safety and rape is a must. Many of our students are socially naive and want to fit in, which can make them easy targets. Most campuses have student escort services to walk students home after a late-night on-campus activity – your daughter should be required to use this. Just as when she was younger, it is important to have discussions about such issues as accepting drinks from strangers, letting unknown individuals into the residence hall, and keeping aware when walking alone. *These issues do not apply only to women; male students can also be the target of assault and rape.*

Many of our students with AS are gullible and trusting, making them easy targets for teasing and jokes.

Bullying

Colleges do not tolerate bullying anywhere on campus, no matter who the instigator is. Whenever students mingle with their peers, there is this potential for bullying ... from either party. Many of our students with AS don't dress, act, or talk like typical students – and they have been emotionally and verbally attacked when others can discover power only by teasing. Groups of students have even gone to the lengths of picking on students with AS in cyberspace. FaceBook sites have been set up to showcase students and their differences.

We strongly suggest you speak frankly with the residence staff and Disability Services about the culture on campus. Students must know there are safe people and safe places and that you and Disability Services will work together to help them locate those resources. Just as we "bully proofed" our kids when they were in middle school, we want to encourage students who have been the target of bullying to bring it to someone's attention so that the situation can be investigated and rectified. Bullying of vulnerable students should not be tolerated on college campuses. (We discuss safety later in this chapter.)

Less obvious bullying takes the form of being taken advantage of in groups, doing all the work for a project or assignment or being excluded from the work a group is doing. Again, encourage your student to feel comfortable bringing this up to his or her point person or another safe person so that the situation can be investigated and the student can be advised on how best to handle it.

Online Safety

The online community is a source of grave threat to young students. We hope that you have discussed online safety with your student. Not just as a one-time event but as an ongoing theme. College students communicate

Many of our students with AS don't dress, act, or talk like typical students – and they have been emotionally and verbally attacked when others can discover power only by teasing.

through social networking sites, and it is recommended that our students on the spectrum be familiar with this medium.

A thorough discussion of this topic is well beyond the scope of this book. However, we suggest that parents and professionals work with the students to understand that there may be dangers inherent in online communities and that they understand how to protect their identity, their confidential information, and their online profile.

Fire Alarms and Safety Drills

In addition to being disorienting, to some students on the spectrum fire drills are not viewed as an activity of value because at the moment there is no fire to be concerned about – in addition, their prior experience in high school probably showed them that fire drills are nothing to worry about. Being woken up in the middle of the night by a noisy alarm and having to go outside may be scary, and may be particularly distressing to a student with more involved sensory issues.

Some students have been known to hide from the noise, burrowing under bedcovers, in closets, etc. If this is a likely occurrence for your student, you must disclose to the RAs so that they can either assign a buddy or otherwise make sure your student is outside with the rest of the students. Providing explicit information about all safety drills, including routes to get out of the building is important, as is being direct and explicit with the student about the need to comply with any and all fire or safety drills.

Laundry and Hygiene

A sure way to have social problems as a college student is to never wash one's clothes or oneself. It is important to remember that it is not the job of Disability Services to teach daily living skills. Students should be routinely taking care of their own hygiene needs and doing their own laundry without prompts before they leave home, so these tasks are not unfamiliar once they are away at college.

You can help the student set a schedule to do his laundry, shower, and perform other acts of hygiene. This can be programmed into a cell phone, personal digital assistant (PDA), or computer, reminding the student to attend to these important tasks of daily living. A run-through when visiting the residence hall to locate the laundry rooms and how to swipe the key card to pay, if applicable, would be useful to be sure students are comfortable with the space and the routine. Also, prearranged times to do laundry when the room is less crowded and students do not have to worry about having their clothes moved or messed with may be useful. Finally, laundry services are an option should all else fail!

Some students are uncomfortable showering around others. It may be possible to help them find a time when there are fewer people in the residence hall (during the middle of the day or late at night tend to be times when fewer students are in the bathrooms). There may also be a more private shower the student can have access to, perhaps in the gym.

Finally, the student who absolutely cannot share a bathroom because he is shy or averse to being in the bathroom with others may require a room with a private bathroom to function successfully. Be aware that this may have implications for room type, size, location, and price so families should explore these variables carefully.

Students should be routinely taking care of their own hygiene needs and doing their own laundry without prompts for a year or more before they leave home, so these tasks are not unfamiliar.

Sleep/Wake Cycle

Some college students sleep all day and are awake all night, while others only sleep for brief periods of time. Many students wake up extremely early in the morning and need stimulation of sorts. This can cause problems in shared living situations. Certainly, in the negotiation of room rules, sleep time and awake time should be discussed.

Some students have asked that blackout shades be installed (or sought permission to install their own) to keep a room dark at all times. This cannot be imposed on a roommate who does not like darkness at all hours, but it is an example of an area of negotiation for the roommate contract. Sleep difficulties may constitute one of the best reasons to consider a single room for the good of your student, as it is not a good plan to face college on little or no sleep.

Sensory Issues

You may have thought that some of your student's sensory sensitivities had gone away; however, they may reappear in the context of a residence hall or shared living environment. Some continue to be hyper-(over) or hypo-(under) sensitive to input from all of their senses. Sights, smells, sounds, and tastes may be extremely exaggerated and even painful due to the differences in processing information.

To combat sensory issues, many students use certain obsessive rituals. For example, a student may follow a certain route to class to avoid lights or smells or return to the residence hall during the middle of the day to take a shower when the noise of dryers and razors is not so overwhelming. Taste and touch are constantly evident from the dining halls to crowded hallways. For students with sensory integration issues, this can be overwhelming.

You may have thought that some of your student's sensory sensitivities had gone away; however, they may reappear in the context of a residence hall or shared living environment.

Lights and classroom noise, such as that from air conditioners and heaters, or fans on LCD projectors, can be physically painful. The sound and smell of markers on a white board or chalk on a blackboard can also cause a physical reaction.

In the residence hall, sensory issues may become extra critical when it comes to the noise and crowding during fire alarms or lockdowns. Be sure your student knows what to do in a fire alarm or lockdown and how to deal with the high degree of stimulation that is inevitable at such times. This is an essential discussion to have with an RD if your student has difficulty with noise and crowds such as everyone leaving the residence hall in a fire alarm. Be sure to work out alternate plans or a buddy system. Some of our students have done well when given a job or task such as being an assistant in fire alarms and drills. This gives the student certain fixed responsibilities and guidelines to follow and, therefore, feels more in control in this sort of situation.

Students with severe sensory issues work hard to keep control when their senses are bombarded. Imagine how difficult it might be to attend to academic learning while trying to remain calm in an overwhelming sensory environment. Having a peaceful room to retreat to may be a means of survival.

In response to sensory overload, many students with AS engage

Students with severe sensory issues work hard to keep control when their senses are bombarded. Imagine how difficult it might be to attend to academic learning while trying to remain calm in an overwhelming sensory environment.

in a behavior colloquially known as "stimming." You know your youngster's stims, and you recall that the stims escalate under periods of stress. In adults, stims might include pacing, finger flicking, muttering, rocking, and fiddling with objects. Stims serve an adaptive purpose and should not be forbidden. Stims reduce anxiety and enhance focus for some students. However, they may be somewhat stigmatizing when done in public, and students may need either a single room or a quiet familiar place on campus where they can de-stress and stim without fear of being observed. When sensory issues arise in the classroom, we have successfully advocated that students be allowed to bring sensory gadgets to class rather than leaving their seat to wander around the classroom.

Residence Staff Training

Many of the problems that arise for students on the spectrum occur in the residence hall rather than in the classroom. Many students with AS exhibit most of their unique behaviors in the residence halls. Their room becomes their home and, as we know, students exhibit more behaviors at home than in school. At home (now the campus room), students should be able to let down their guard and allow behaviors they usually control in "public."

We advocate specialized training for residence life and have successfully trained a number of campuses so that their resident staff can appreciate and facilitate this without being unduly alarmed.

We advocate specialized training and have successfully trained a number of campuses so that their residence staff can appreciate and facilitate such behaviors without being unduly alarmed. Though residence hall staff cannot be informed about specific students without a student's consent, RAs may be trained to recognize some of the difficulties of living in residence halls and in community living and how to assist students with AS. Depending on the campus, Disability Services may or may not be able to speak freely with residence staff until or unless a crisis occurs, in which case the need to know may override strict confidentiality. But understand that the staff in the residence hall are trained to deal with a range of student issues and welcome information about your student so that they can facilitate his or her integration into residence life.

In this chapter we outlined some of the important things you need to know if you are (or considering in future) transitioning your student to a residential college where he or she will be living in shared space. It is doable but requires preparation on the part of the student and the family. This aspect of college life should not be the one you leave until the week before move-in! In the next chapter we will discuss how and where your student will go to keep healthy.

Andrew made a friend this year. Sam lived in the same residence hall as Andrew; he was a nice, quiet guy, and he did not make Andrew nervous. They went to meals together sometimes and once to a movie. Sam studied a lot, just like Andrew. They were both going to be juniors, and Sam asked Andrew if he wanted to room together the next year in the new luxury dorm that was only for upper-classmen. By pooling their lottery numbers, they were able to score a suite! The only problem was it was comprised of a double room, a single room, common space, and one bathroom.

Andrew really needed his single and was worried about talking to Sam about it. He finally worked up his courage. When they talked about it, Sam said it was fine – he would take the double and invited another guy into the suite who had a girlfriend on another campus whom he visited frequently.

CHAPTER 11

Student Health –
Physical and Mental

Luke could not get out of bed. The alarm rang and rang, the snooze had gone off so many times that he finally just turned it off. He had class in 20 minutes. He would probably be late anyway, so why even go.

Luke had not left his room in three days. He ate what was in his mini-fridge and some granola bars, he had bottled water and some Gatorade. He was fine for another day. He felt tired all the time, couldn't concentrate on his work, and didn't want to talk to anyone. His mom kept calling, but he didn't answer. Why can't everybody just leave him alone?

In the previous chapter, we introduced information and strategies for your student to learn to live on campus, with or without a roommate. As part of becoming adult and assuming independent living skills, your student must know how to take care of himself and where to turn for help should he become ill. In previous chapters, we encouraged you to make this part of the transition process well before your student moved to campus. We will now discuss in more depth what he will need to know and do.

I t is sometimes easier for students to get in to see a doctor on campus than it is to see your local doctor. Most colleges have a walk-in health service on campus, and most services are covered by the school's mandatory health insurance. Some small schools have a nurse on campus during the day, with a doctor on call and local hospitals ready for more serious illnesses. Large universities have sophisticated health services with touch-screen triage service and self-service over-the-counter pharmacies and prescription pharmacies.

All this is worthless, of course, unless students know how to access the services. Has your student ever had to take himself to the doctor without you?

As a basic condition for living away from home safely, students with AS *absolutely must* know how to report medical issues and be able to interact with health professionals (nurse, nurse practitioner, physician's assistant, and physician). These skills should be practiced prior to the college transition.

Some of the key issues students must understand about being responsible for their own health care include
- when to go to the doctor
- how to explain their symptoms once in the doctor's office
- how to care for themselves after the appointment in terms of medications, what reactions to watch out for, followup appointments, etc.

When to Go to the Doctor

Students with AS may be so accustomed to being told what to do and when to do it that figuring out things like whether they are sick and what to do about it is very difficult. Also, students with AS may be more (hyper-) or less (hypo-) sensitive to how their body feels.

As parents we must teach our young adults to recognize signs of physical or mental illness and to listen to their body and get help when needed. As for many other skills, they need practice.

Your family doctor may be able to assist in preparing your student. Further, you can role-play with the student. Does she understand her body and how to know when she is not well? Does she understand how to report severity of symptoms or does she under-report? Does she know what to say to a doctor at the health center?

As a basic condition for living away from home safely, students with AS absolutely must know how to report medical issues and be able to interact with health professionals

An especially useful tool is a laminated emergency card listing symptoms that require a doctor's visit pasted on the mirror or door of the student's room.

How to Explain Their Symptoms

Students with AS are usually so well understood by their parents that doctor's visits consist of much talking of the parents and little talking by the young person with AS. (This can also stem from communication and other pragmatic functioning issues.)

When the child with AS reaches high school age, he or she must begin to practice the skills of using health care professionals. Give your daughter or son time to talk to the doctor, nurse, nurse practitioner, or physician's assistant. Young people need to learn to ask questions and report symptoms on their own. Then the parent can follow up about additional concerns.

Caring for Themselves After the Appointment

Going to health services will not be worthwhile if the student does not know how to follow the doctor's (or health care professional's) advice after the appointment. By the time he leaves home, the student must be able independently to have prescriptions filled, take medicine according to instructions, make healthy choices in food and snacks, exercise, etc.

Give your student these opportunities while he is still in high school so that he may better succeed independently later on. One responsibility added at a time (maybe one per month or per season) will make this a gradual and, therefore, not such an overwhelming transition for everybody involved.

Medical Leave of Absence

There are circumstances in which a medical or mental health problem becomes a reason for leave of absence. When a student is in crisis, our preferred route is to first work with the family and the student on a reduced course load or perhaps adding accommodations or support. But when the problem has interfered with attendance and keeping up with work to the extent that the student falls too far behind (as in weeks to a month), or when the problem is either unresolved or resolving too slowly despite doctor visits, medications, or therapy, a medical leave of absence is often the best option.

A medical leave of absence can prevent the student's grade point average (GPA) from plummeting due to a semester of bad grades as a result of illness and missed classes. A medical leave of absence may also preserve the student's eligibility for continued health insurance (depending on the nature of the parent's plan). Finally, a leave can also salvage a student's self-esteem – high expectations are a large part of the personality of the student with AS.

Contacting Disability Services can be the beginning of the leave of absence request. On some campuses, such leaves are granted by the Dean of Students or some other Student Affairs office. Regardless, Disability Services can get the student connected to the right person or begin the process with the student.

It is extremely important that medical leaves of absence be handled officially, as the student's health insurance and student loans may be tied to their status as a full time student. A letter to the insurance company or bank explaining that the student is on an official medical leave of absence may be necessary.

By the time he leaves home, the student must be able independently to have prescriptions filled, take medicine according to instructions, make healthy choices in food and snacks, exercise, etc.

Mental Health

Co-existing psychiatric diagnoses are common in AS, especially anxiety disorders and depression. If your student falls in this category, you know how difficult it can be. If your student has not previously struggled with mental health problems in addition to AS, you may find yourself in unfamiliar territory should stress and loneliness overwhelm him or her in college. This section will prepare you to better navigate these issues.

Emotions

There is a common misperception that individuals with AS are cold or unemotional. Those of us who live with them know this is far from the case! Your student with AS may become easily overwhelmed and may have low frustration tolerance levels. He may be fearful and anxious because he does not always integrate information, because of sensory overload, because he feels lost in space, or because of social confusion. There may be a disconnect between his output (in terms of behavior, performance) and his intent and the expectations of others, which can also lead to frustration, confusion, or anxiety. Your student may be prone to anxiety disorders with

There is a common misperception that individuals with AS are cold or unemotional. Those of us who live with them know this is far from the case!

or without panic attacks, including obsessive compulsive disorder, social anxiety disorder, and generalized anxiety disorders. Internalizing psychopathology, depression, and even suicide, are commonly experienced, particularly in adolescents and young adults. In adolescence, the expectation for more sophisticated social skills on top of increasing academic demands can be overwhelming. In high school, the student with AS may be marginalized, becoming more withdrawn and isolated. Difficulty fitting in with the right crowd and understanding how to dress, ask for a date, or be "cool" can be demoralizing.

All this sets the stage for onset of feelings of depression and signal that it is time to get help before things become worse. When such feelings are present in a youngster, his parents are generally there to read the warning signs, but when he has left for college, then what?

Campus Mental Health Services

With the increased focus on mental health, depression, and suicide on college campuses in recent years, most colleges have developed very comprehensive services for assessment, treatment, and/or referral both on and off campus. Many students with AS would benefit from counseling services, but they may find the many configurations of counseling centers and the services they provide to be confusing. Families experience this confusion as well. A large campus may have multiple similar-sounding clinics, including research clinics and training facilities. On some campuses, mental health services provide counseling while the counseling center is for emergencies. On other campuses, there is one office that provides all the services.

It is important to find out the particulars of your campus to be sure that should a mental health crisis emerge, the student can quickly get to the appropriate office. The office of Disability Services is a good place to start. In terms of treatment, some campuses have a session limit, while others offer unlimited services. Parents, students, and clinicians from the student's hometown should be aware of these limits before they assume that ongoing mental health care is going to be provided at the expected level. If your son has been receiving weekly therapy and monthly medication checks, find out if the campus can provide this level of care or if an off-campus referral for long-term treatment is necessary.

Please consider this as a necessity for everyone's peace of mind. Research this well before you pack the car to leave. Students and their families need time to adjust to changes in providers, and you do not want this to be sprung on the student at the last minute when he is stressed, or worse yet, find there is no one prepared to see him.

Stress Management

Students with AS who are very affected by stress and anxiety often need continued counseling support from the outset of their college career. It is crucial to know what can precipitate a crisis, how stress manifests itself, and what behaviors to look for.

Spend the time before your student leaves home to review what sort of events have triggered stress reactions in the past. Was it sensory overload? Rejection by a peer? Academic stress? Holidays? Changes in surroundings? Unpredictability? Is the student aware of these triggers? Does she know how to calm herself and know what strategies (including medication) she has taken in the past when stressed?

Students with AS who are very affected by stress and anxiety often need continued counseling support from the outset of their college career.

All of this information can be communicated to Disability Services as well as student mental health as soon as the student moves on to campus or begins classes as a commuter, should the student face any of these triggers during the semester. Standard stress-busting measures are useful and can be particularly helpful if built into the student's schedule as preventive measures.

As a classic stress reducer, exercise increases the chemicals that battle anxiety and depression and have the added benefit of preventing us from getting sick. Exercise can be an excellent study break. Exercise on a campus could be a structured class, a swim, a bike ride, or just a walk.

Another good stress management technique is social activity. On a college campus, even eating meals can be social. Though students with AS have difficulty with social activities, most have a great desire for companionship. Taking breaks from studying to hang out on the floor or in the dining commons can be a great way to reduce stress. If your student's RA knows the student is struggling, he or she can assist with more social inclusion to battle stress. Some students migrate towards more solitary stress-busting activities such as meditation, yoga, or listening to music.

Regardless of what your student prefers, we suggest that you discuss with her in advance how to recognize when she is under stress and what steps she can take to mitigate it. At the very minimum, make sure she has contacted Disability Services and knows to turn there when she can remember no one else.

Please see the a stress management thermometer based on Kari Dunn-Buron's 5-Point Scale (2007). With her permission, we have adapted it for use with college students as a way of identifying potentially troublesome situations they will encounter at college and possible solutions and strategies for de-escalating their stress levels.

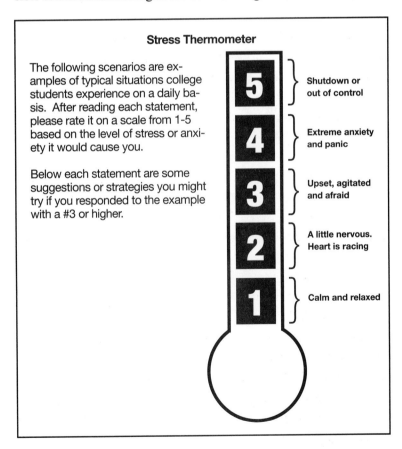

Stress Thermometer

The following scenarios are examples of typical situations college students experience on a daily basis. After reading each statement, please rate it on a scale from 1-5 based on the level of stress or anxiety it would cause you.

Below each statement are some suggestions or strategies you might try if you responded to the example with a #3 or higher.

5 — Shutdown or out of control

4 — Extreme anxiety and panic

3 — Upset, agitated and afraid

2 — A little nervous. Heart is racing

1 — Calm and relaxed

20-Question Stress Test

College Scenarios:

1. The seat you usually sit in is taken when you get to class. ___
   Possible Strategy: If you responded with a 3 or higher, you might try getting to class 5 minutes earlier to make sure you can get the seat you like or have a second choice of seat in mind in case your first choice is taken.

2. The professor has left a note on the classroom door explaining that class will be held in an alternative building today. ___
   Possible Strategy: If you responded with a 3 or higher, you might try some deep breathing for a few minutes, then consult your campus map for the new location. You could also ask somebody for information on how to get there.

3. In class, students are asked to discuss a reading with a student next to you. ___
   Possible Strategy: If you responded with a 3 or higher, you might try saying hello and introducing yourself first and then mention one aspect of the reading that you were interested in.

4. The bookstore does not have the book you need when you arrive to purchase it. ___
   Possible Strategy: If you responded with a 3 or higher, you might try locating a bookstore employee and ask what steps you should take to get the book as soon as possible.

5. Your professor announces a pop quiz when you enter the room. ___
   Possible Strategy: If you responded with a 3 or higher, you might try taking a few calming breaths and reminding yourself that you are intelligent and that all students feel a little nervous when taking pop quizzes. Additionally, remember that pop quizzes generally only count for a small percentage of your grades.

6. Your roommate has eaten something that was in the refrigerator that belonged to you. ___
   Possible Strategy: If you responded with a 3 or higher, you might try writing down the reasons why that was upsetting to you and some ideas for how you would like sharing the refrigerator to work in the future.

7. The campus or public transportation on which you are riding forgets to stop at your bus stop to let you off. ___
   Possible Strategy: If you responded with a 3 or higher, you might try calmly walking to the front of the bus and asking the bus driver politely to take you back to the previous stop. You might also get off at the very next stop instead.

8. You must walk through a very crowded hallway to get to your class-room or dorm room. ___
Possible Strategy: If you responded with a 3 or higher, you might try looking for an alternative way to get there. If it takes longer, you may have to plan for the extra time needed.

9. The grade you get on your first paper (you thought it was A quality) is a C-, and the professor instructs you to see her about it. ___
Possible Strategy: If you responded with a 3 or higher, you might try emailing the instructor to find out if you can make an appoint-ment and when you might do so. Remember that most students feel nervous when meeting their instructors, but instructors are there to help you become a better writer, not to criticize you as a person. Promise yourself you will listen to what they have to say when you meet with them and perhaps write down the suggestions they make.

10. Your roommate has left dirty clothes on your side of the room. ___
Possible Strategy: If you responded with a 3 or higher, you might try politely asking your roommate to please keep their belongings on their part of the room.

11. Your roommate has left a note on the door explaining that he/she has a guest and doesn't want to be disturbed. ___
Possible Strategy: If you responded with a 3 or higher, you might try consulting your hall residence advisor for guidance on how to handle the situation.

12. The night before your first college summer course begins, you notice that the college's academic planner that you purchased does not start until September of the upcoming fall semester.___
Possible Strategy: If you responded with a 3 or higher, you might try contacting Disability Services and asking for suggestions for how to obtain a summer planner.

13. The person in your class whom you followed to the food court in-tending to ask out on a date just told you to back off and stop stalk-ing them. ___
Possible Strategy: If you responded with a 3 or higher, you might try asking a trusted adult for guidance on dating and friendships.

14. When returning to your dorm one night, the doors to the building have been locked and your key does not work.___

Possible Strategy: If you responded with a 3 or higher, you might try putting your college's Safety and Security Office number and your residence hall advisor's number into your cell phone so that you can call them should this happen.

15. When you enter one of your classes for the first time, you are immediately overwhelmed by the fluorescent lights, the smell of chemicals in the room, and sound of the projector fan. ___
   Possible Strategy: If you responded with a 3 or higher, you might try stepping outside the room for a few minutes to settle down and decide whether to approach the instructor and/or call your Disability Services specialist for ideas on how to proceed.

16. Your residence advisor tells you there have been complaints about your hygiene. ___
   Possible Strategy: If you responded with a 3 or higher, you might try asking your RA for assistance in adding time and tasks related to keeping good hygiene to your daily schedule.

17. They are out of the only foods you like when you get to the dining hall. ___
   Possible Strategy: If you responded with a 3 or higher, you may want to purchase some "emergency foods" to keep in your dorm or refrigerator so you will have something to eat on those occasions.

18. The electricity goes off in your residence hall during a severe storm. ___
   Possible Strategy: If you responded with a 3 or higher, take a few minutes to calm yourself, then consider calling out for assistance from your RA., roommate or peer. Keep a flashlight in your room where you can locate it in any future occurance.

19. The student down the hall turns up his stereo full blast after you have gone to bed. ___
   Possible Strategy: If you responded with a 3 or higher, you could calmly ask the the student to please turn it down. You could also ask for guidance from your RA.

20. There are no showers available when you have planned your schedule precisely. ___
   Possible Strategy: If you responded with a 3 or higher, check your schedule to see if you can move another activity to accommodate taking your shower at a different time.

Medications

Many students come to campus with a history of various medications taken for problems with focus, self-injurious behavior, or depression. If your student is going away to college, it is vital that you arrange ahead of time to have a medical professional in place for followup.

Students must have a medical contact in the area where they attend college so that a health professional has their full history and can prescribe medications during the transition. This is especially important in case of emergencies (e.g., while adjusting to a new routine, the student takes his meds in the bathroom and accidentally drops a bottle of meds down the sink).

Your student must be instructed on what she takes, what the dosage is – in other words how to take medications responsibly without adult supervision. A medication monitor in the residence hall or at student health is not available, so it is incumbent on parents and treating professionals to ensure that the student knows how and when to take her medications, what side effects to monitor, and how to get prescriptions refilled when needed. The student also needs to know how to keep medication safe, especially if she is taking stimulant medications or other meds commonly used as "study aides." Your physician needs to have a candid conversation with the student about the risks and penalties of misusing medications.

Crisis Intervention

Crisis behavior may be seen as students not going to class, not leaving their room, or having outbursts. For some students, the crisis behavior is more inward – they stay in their room and socialize even less than before. Depending on your student, it may take the form of more calls home – or fewer.

If you suspect your student is in crisis, do not let it go unaddressed. When the student is experiencing a crisis, ideally, a staff member (perhaps in residence life, in Disability Services, on in the Dean of Students office) is notified by the student, a peer, or another staff or faculty member. If the student has established a relationship with a counselor on or off campus already, this relationship will be very helpful at these times. Colleges usually use a local hospital or on campus psychiatrist for immediate treatment. Of course, if the student is in any danger, a hospitalization or emergency room treatment will be necessary.

The following table lists examples of potentially concerning behaviors and the most likely staff person to contact.

Crisis Intervention	
Examples of Behaviors That Can Be a Cause for Concern	**Potential Staff to Contact**
Self-injurious behavior: cutting, picking at skin, pulling out hair, etc.	• Residence life director or RA on student's floor • If student is connected with Disability Services, contact student's provider • Counseling Center • Dean of Students
Change in daily living routine: increase or decrease in sleep, rapid weight gain or loss, increase in hygiene issues	Same as above. If institution has a health and wellness center, this may also be a good office to contact
Missed classes, increase or decrease in communication with you through email, phone, texts, etc.	• RA • Student's academic advisor • Disability Services • Dean of Students
Increase in stress management behaviors: flapping, talking to oneself, increase in computer game playing	• RA • Student's roommate or friends • Disability Services • Health and Wellness • Counseling
Manic-type behaviors: extreme high or low energy, grandiosity, extreme spending, extreme fatigue, etc.	• Residence life director • Counseling • Dean of Students
Suicidal talk or ideas	• Counseling • Dean of Students • Security
Note. This table is not meant to be exhaustive. These behaviors may occur in isolation, but most likely in some combination. You know your student best and indications that she may be in trouble.	**Note.** If your student has not signed a release of information form to the above individuals prior to your call, they may not be able to share information with you or acknowledge if they work with your son or daughter. However, that does not mean that they do not take your concerns seriously.

It is important to spend some time with your student and his or her clinicians to figure out what event could have precipitated the crisis as this may be useful in assisting the student and averting future crises. Sometimes a break from school and a long weekend at home is enough to help. At other times, a leave of absence may be required until the student's condition stabilizes.

Medical and Mental Health Backup

Though mental health services are available on campus, it is important for some students with AS to have support from medical and mental health professionals off campus. For example, a student with AS begins college and needs a prescription filled. He cannot get his medications, and there is a two-week wait for an intake appointment with a psychiatrist on campus. Needless to say, he cannot wait that long. Therefore, having an established relationship with a physician in the area prior to the start of the semester is recommended.

What Should Disability Services Know About Mental Health?

Optimally, you and your son or daughter have agreed to send the Disability Services office all relevant medical and psychiatric information as soon as a decision is made on which school to attend, so that they can properly accommodate any issues that arise. Do not be reticent about disclosing such conditions as depression, obsessive-compulsive disorder, or aggressive behavior. Understand that this information is not shared unless the (adult) student consents to disseminate information, and it does not go on a transcript. Most families are willing to disclose psychiatric information when they see how important such information becomes in ensuring the student's academic success along with physical and mental well-being on campus.

In this chapter we discussed physical and emotional health and what students need to be able to do to keep themselves healthy, and what to do when they do not feel well. In the next chapter, we will discuss how students keep themselves active and happy, and how to strike the sometimes elusive balance between work and play.

Eric doesn't want to go talk to this counselor again, but he knows that if he doesn't go to the appointment, the counselor has permission to call his parents. According to their arrangement, if Eric misses his counseling appointments, he has to withdraw from school for the semester. Eric does not want to do that, so he goes to the counselor every week. Though he does not like going, he has to admit he feels a little bit better after talking to her, and meeting with his counselor keeps his parents from nagging him. He even thinks they sometimes talk about good stuff – like how to be more comfortable if he tries to join clubs and introduce himself.

CHAPTER 12

Social and Extracurricular Life

Molly had met another student in her biology class. She seems nice; she even talked to Molly about class, labs, and other things going on at school. Molly thinks they might become friends. The other student asked Molly to join her and some other friends at dinner in the dining hall that night. Molly wants to go, but the dining hall makes her so nervous – all those people, the noise, and the smells, she just can't think or talk in there, let alone eat. That night at dinner time, Molly can't bring herself to go to the dining hall and meet her classmate. Now she doesn't know if the girls will all talk mean about her, and what will she say to the student in class – perhaps she will not like her now that she didn't show up for dinner.

Only a fraction of a student's time each day is spent in class, and for students with AS difficulties often arise in navigating interactions out of class. Housing and residence life pose special challenges, as does the social milieu of a campus.

Student Life staff and higher education professionals refer to what occurs outside the classroom as "co-curricular," encompassing residence life, student activities, Greek life, religious life, athletics, and cultural events on campus. As a complement to the academic experience, even students who struggle with social disabilities need to be encouraged to participate. Don't let your student come home each weekend because there is nothing to do on campus – there is always something to do on campus!

Colleges and universities go to great lengths to program and facilitate activities – clubs, sports, shows, movies, gatherings, meals, you name it – designed specifically to engage all students in the life of the campus. In this chapter, we will introduce some of the activities students can get involved in once they have arrived on campus as well as specific strategies your son or daughter can use to get comfortable with the social life at their school.

Student Activities

Student activities are important to the overall mental health and happiness of all students. All of the recognized campus clubs, activities, organizations, outings, even intramural sports, are categorized under Student Activities. Informal clubs are often formed by students with common interests as well. Both structured (i.e., organized by the students and/or the university) and unstructured (hanging out, dating) activities are important components of the nonacademic experience for all students. Having one or two activities outside the classroom can add needed structure to the student's weekly schedule and increase social opportunities.

For many students with AS, co-curricular activities are some of the biggest challenges on campus. But there is help. Where it is a good match, we encourage students to participate in special interest clubs such as the chess club or animé club. Particularly on large campuses, there are hundreds of clubs, and one of them is sure to be a good (if not perfect) match to the special interests the student may have. For example, dungeons and dragons groups, genealogy groups, and film clubs are often good matches.

Another excellent choice for students who do not make friends easily and who are daunted by the prospect of going to a club meeting cold is an organized service activity, such as tutoring elementary school students, or becoming involved in a recycling program or a social justice activity. Working together with like-minded people of similar age on a project with clear goals is a great ice breaker and effective means for students with AS to become more comfortable socializing with peers.

For many students with AS, co-curricular activities are some of the biggest challenges on campus.

The list below is only a sampling of what might be attractive to your student. Some campuses offer more than 500 student clubs, and as many shows, concerts, and other entertainment opportunities in a semester. Check out the Student Activities websites at your campus.

Examples of Social Activities (Other Than Parties)

- Clubs and special interest groups
- Study groups
- Dances
- Greek life (fraternities and sororities)
- Athletics (intramural and club sports or spectator)
- Religious life
- Political activities
- Community service
- Performing arts
- On-campus jobs

Dating

Most of our students express an interest in meeting a partner on campus. Indeed, that goal is one of the markers of adult transition. However, even the most skilled of students with AS may be at an impasse in terms of dating on campus. Traditional 1:1 dating seems to be a thing of the past, with most students today hanging out, dating in groups, or "hooking up." Dates are often made through social networking, and our students may not understand this medium well enough to comprehend when they are being asked to participate.

If your student made friends or dated in high school, he will likely do just fine with a little guidance. But if your student was a loner, he will likely require some social mentoring. You may want to have a trusted young adult (a friend or relative perhaps) explain some of this to him. Our general advice is that students join a club or other group activity as a way to meet people.

We understand that there are impediments to socializing in the makeup of many of our students, and that lack of success in this area is not simply due to the fact that they are shy or lazy.

Barriers to Social Activity

We understand that there are impediments to socializing in the makeup of many of our students, and that lack of success in this area is not simply due to the fact that they are shy or lazy. We will turn to some of the reasons some of our students may struggle with achieving a satisfying social life.

Cognitive Challenges

Cognitive challenges such as inflexibility or rigid thinking can impact the student as she attempts to navigate the social climate of the college or university. The student may have difficulty organizing her room, keeping track of belongings, or remembering the various routes between classroom buildings, residence halls, and dining halls.

A vital role for parents is to become familiar with all the new and potentially confusing procedures, clarify them to the student, and practice, practice, practice. Together, you can prepare reminders to be posted in the student's room or carried in wallets or backpacks. High-tech re-minders can be programmed into the ever-present cell phone if the student is tech savvy. Reminders can include meal times, studying in the library (as opposed to alone in the residence hall), exercise time, movie time, and other opportunities for social interaction.

Miles has found an animé club that he enjoys, but it is difficult for him to make it there each week. His counselor suggested he program it into his smart phone. Each Friday at 4:45, an icon and the theme song from his favorite cartoon pop up, and Miles knows he has 30 minutes to cross campus, get a snack, and make it to the club meeting.

Behavioral Challenges

In order to gain the most from the college experience, students need to get involved with life outside the classroom – organizations and the broader campus community. But many students with AS are afraid of these new experiences, and many simply do not know how to go about finding, joining, and participating

For some, the barriers stem from their own behaviors that are odd or inappropriate like stimming, pacing, nose picking, muttering, etc. Other students may find such behavior gross, odd, or weird. This is not a new reality to your student; most likely, someone in middle or high school was unkind in calling attention to the behavior. Students are often painfully aware that others find them odd, and this can be used as an incentive for them to learn to tone the behavior down. Many youngsters have learned to control their behavior until they are in a safe or quiet space where they can engage in it undisturbed.

In cases where a student's behavior is off-putting to others, discuss with him how to better meet his needs for calming or expressing frus-tration. Someone in Student life, the residence hall, or Disability Services can assist in finding quiet nooks where he can de-escalate without being observed. If the situation is very prominent, the student might benefit from a single room, as discussed in Chapter 10.

Mentoring

Parents often inquire whether their student can be matched up with a sympathetic peer to guide him or her socially on campus. With the exception of campuses where formal mentoring programs are in place, this is not a service that most campuses provide.

Some schools have a social skills group where students where members can meet other students with AS or similar challenges. Other schools have social mentors who meet students on a regular basis to have a meal or do something social together. If your campus offers social mentoring (or even if it doesn't), we encourage you and your student to ask! Generally, someone in the Disability Services office will be the most knowledgeable person to turn to.

We send our kids to college for more than academic reasons. In this chapter, we looked at ways to support them in enjoying other aspects of college, with particular emphasis on social interactions. But we also want them to gain the necessary skills to move on to the world of work. Supportive employment during college is one of the most effective means to train students in both job skills and the so-called "soft" skills they will need after college. In the next chapter, we will present some strategies that will move them in that direction.

Alicia was alone in her room many nights. Her RA was perceptive and suggested that Alicia accompany her to a rally that was happening that afternoon. When they got there, there was a small group of students wearing yellow T-shirts and carrying clipboards. They were handing out leaflets announcing a new sustainability initiative on campus. Alicia had always been interested in global warming and environmental issues, and she thought the kids looked nice. One of the kids came up, and they got to talking. Soon the other girl invited Alicia to come to the next organizational meeting, stating that they needed someone with good organizational skills and attention to detail to keep the minutes of their meetings. Alicia plans to go next week.

CHAPTER 13

Life After College

Andrew is a second-semester senior. He has worked very hard in his college career and has a good grade point average. He has had a few summer job experiences doing landscaping and scooping ice cream but has no professional experience. He knows his college years are ending, but he does not know what to do after graduation.

The process of looking for a job, writing a resume, getting clothes appropriate for a job interview and even a voice-mail message appropriate for prospective employers are things his parents and Career Services have talked to him about. Andrew can barely keep up with his academic requirements, how can he think about all these other things? It's overwhelming and causes him to melt down for hours when he thinks about it all.

Most of us agree with the truism that going to college is supposed to better our kids' chances of getting a job and becoming independent adults. We want nothing more than for our kids with AS to be self-sustaining and happily (or at least gainfully) employed. But how are they going to make this leap? A detailed plan for employment preparation is beyond the scope of this book, but it is not too early to begin to think about employment skills as your student navigates college.

In this chapter, we will explore some of the important skills your student will need to master in order to be a good employee. Skills such as phone etiquette, timeliness, managing emotions, reporting to an authority figure are not innate skills – someone has to teach our students how to behave on the job.

Why Work During College?

Job experience is crucial to a student's future employability. For many students with AS, internships, externships, or co-op experiences are key to getting jobs after college since many students come to college with no prior job experience. Perhaps their time has been filled with after-school therapies or tutoring. Perhaps you as the parent have felt protective of their summer down time. Perhaps they could not have handled the logistics of getting and going to a job.

If students are to learn the important skills for work before actually taking their first "real" job, it needs to happen before they graduate from college. By gaining these skills within the college environment, students feel more supported and get more guidance in understanding the socially complex world of work. While young workers who have been fired believe the reason was related to lack of skills or connections, it has been reported that one of the main reasons is the inability to get along with co-workers (http://www. finaid.wwu.edu/studentjobs/students/resources/job_behaviors.php)

While colleges generally think of post-graduation gainful employment as an acknowledgment of successful completion of the undergraduate degree program, for parents of students with AS the matter of employment is fraught with concerns and doubts – another chapter of life laced with hidden land mines. Until colleges and universities become more experienced at supporting students with AS and anticipating the accommodations they need, the task of nudging them through the process falls to parents, and the work of preparing these students for gainful employment by colleges must begin much earlier.

It is extremely important that AS students take full advantage of any opportunities to work that are made available at their colleges. The information we provide here is intended to arm parents with insight on how the college can best prepare the student with AS with skills that will make the transition to gainful employment after graduation more successful

For many students with AS, internships, externships, or co-op experiences are key to getting jobs after college since many students come to college with no prior job experience.

Transitioning to On-Campus Work

College students' thoughts generally turn toward jobs searches during their final academic year (even though college career offices have much to offer all students). However, the student with AS is best advised to begin preparing for work much earlier, ideally, during the sophomore year of studies. The experience of working and the knowledge gained about a field of interest are immeasurable.

Such experiences may be earned via such options as …

- externship – temporary position in an agency that has agreed to provide work experience to a student, often without pay
- internship – work experience associated with a student's field of study, often without pay
- co-op – work experience in the student's field of study for which the student is paid

Besides a safe environment, these various options give unique opportunities for support and learning about the work environment. Indeed, an internship or other types of field placement may be the optimal time to get feedback as an employee.

The student with AS is best advised to begin preparing for work much earlier, ideally, during the sophomore year of studies.

Many colleges and universities have educational units such as internship departments or cooperative education departments that are designed to broaden students' awareness of the various types of work environments they are likely to find after graduation. Some schools have developed protocols for students with social skills disorders like AS that focus on helping students learn about the work culture and acquire solid work skills that will enable them to fit better into the work culture.

Some families turn to vocational rehabilitation services support for assistance in providing the student with job readiness skills. Vocational rehabilitation agencies exist in each state to support individuals with disabilities who require either acquisition of job readiness skills or placement in an agency that has agreed to provide more intensive support of sponsored employees through collaboration with the vocational rehabilitation agency.

As a parent of a college student, you can help your son or daughter become aware of the standards that generally hold true regardless of the culture or type of employment he or she ends up in. The following are examples of such standards. They are important fundamental principles for AS students to learn and integrate.

General Work-Related Standards

- Arrive to work on time
- Know and observe the company's policy concerning illness-related absences
- Know and observe the company's policy about eating at one's desk
- Observe the company's dress code and adopt it
- Meet deadlines
- Do not make personal phone calls at work
- Do not play computer games at your work station
- Know whom you must address more formally

While an introduction to the range and variety of work setting types and cultures serves as a valuable way to gain baseline information, its primary purpose is to provide a knowledge base from which the student can begin to build awareness of increasingly more subtle issues. The goal is to arm the student with knowledge, tools, and skills that he can apply at each work setting in which he finds himself, with the interim goal being identification of appropriate behaviors in each new job setting, and the ultimate goal being successful survival in the work world after graduation.

Student Employment

We firmly believe that every student, with AS or not, should work on campus at some point in their college careers. In addition to the satisfaction of earning money and the accompanying opportunity to learn money management, such an experience gives young people much-needed lessons in the modern workplace and provides them an opportunity to work alongside more skilled professionals who can serve as mentors.

A professor in whose class they did well may be looking for a lab assistant. The library may need a quiet student to shelve books. The Disability Services office may need computer literate individuals to input data. The IT department may need students to staff the help desks.

We firmly believe that every student, AS or not, should work on campus at some point in their college careers.

Do not let your student overlook the importance of talking to someone in the student employment office that is usually associated with the Financial Aid office to search for on-campus work opportunities.

Career Services

Career Services is the office on campus that is officially charged with assisting with employment, usually construed as securing a job after graduation. But these professional career counselors can also assist with selecting majors, narrowing interests and aspirations, as well as assisting with pre-graduation placement in internships or co-op jobs. If the career counselor understands that the student is on the spectrum, he or she may be able to work with the student to find a job that would be a good fit for the student's interests, skills, and unique characteristics. The counselor may also be able to assist with developing good interviewing skills as well as creating an effective resume. Therefore, your student may want to provide the career counselor with information about the characteristics that set him apart from his peers (positive as well as negative). He or she should be sure to focus on social skills, as well as any needs for specific assistance in interpreting their environment, project/time management, and interviewing.

Ferreting out employers who are flexible enough to be accepting of employees who need support and understanding is critical to a successful placement and a positive work experience for students with AS. Agencies that receive federal grants and contracts may be more responsive, given that they have had long-standing obligations to hire individuals with disabilities, dating back to the introduction of Section 504 of the Rehabilitation Act of 1973. Some of these companies have a person in the Affirmative Action office or a human resource manager who is responsible for outreach in hiring individuals with disabilities and supporting them once they are on

Ferreting out employers who are flexible enough to be accepting of employees who need support and understanding is critical to a successful placement and a positive work experience for students with AS.

the job. You may also need to work with the vocational rehabilitation services in your region for assistance with locating employers who have a commitment to providing work experience to students with disabilities and are agreeable to providing the type of support that may be necessary.

Disclosure

The question of whether students with AS should disclose their disability during the job interview is an important one. In cases where students' social skills are significantly weak and their insights about how to handle themselves in unfamiliar situations are poor, disclosure could mean the difference between being accepted for a position or internship and being rejected because potential employers might mistakenly conclude that their social awkwardness reflects a general incompetence on the part of applicants when that is, in fact, not the case. Thus, disclosure could mean that the potential employer can shift his or her attention to assessing the background skills the student brings to the position and not just focus on her social awkwardness.

Career counselors can work with the students to help them develop ways to disclose their disability in a way that is comfortable to both the worker and the employer. For example, we have advised students to begin the discussion with a general statement referring to the issue as "social dyslexia" as this is a non-pejorative statement that allows for a general discussion about "difficulty reading people."

Particularly in the case of students who have had no previous work experience and need support of a concrete nature to ensure integration into the workforce, parents should work with the student to investigate the extent to which the college can provide job readiness skill development prior to employment or participation in an internship or co-op experience. Often Career Services departments provide such opportunities through periodic workshops.

Some students will need more intensive on-the-job support in order to maximize their job experience. Working with the state vocational rehabilitation agency sufficiently in advance of the anticipated work experience would be key to a successful internship or co-op work experience. In the absence of any support from either the school or other agency, we encourage parents to hire a job coach. This individual should spend time in the agency with the student to assist with smooth integration, interpreting confusing or unfamiliar situations.

Getting Things Done

One of the big challenges for individuals with AS is organizing their time to maximize productivity. Creating a structure within which to work is an important first step in this challenge. Some jobs come with built-in structure and can be a good fit for students who either are facing their first jobs or still struggle to develop structure independently.

Other jobs are not structured, so the student will generally need to work with a supervisor or coach to learn how to manage their tasks. If the student is in an on-campus job, this is a terrific opportunity to engage their supervisor in some on the job training. Similarly, managing long-term projects can be a challenge. If students have not mastered the process of completing long-term assignments in school, they are bound to face challenges in jobs that involve long-term projects replete with deadlines.

Some students will need more intensive on-the-job support in order to maximize their job experience.

Working with the Disability Services in their schools to acquire solid time and project management skills, students should begin by breaking their projects down step by step and numbering the steps in sequence. Again, on-campus jobs before they go into the higher-stakes marketplace offer great learning opportunities in this respect.

Stress and Anger

There comes a time in every job when an employee experiences stress, but for individuals on the autism spectrum, feelings of stress can be particularly intense and hard to manage. Perhaps he has come up against an issue that he cannot resolve such as a new schedule, task or supervisor. Or perhaps a deadline is quickly approaching and she has not made enough progress in her work to be able to meet it; perhaps he is feeling overwhelmed and is either unable to ask for help or does not know whom to ask.

If the pressure is more than he can bear, the individual with AS may react in several ways:
- Crying (irrespective of gender)
- Muttering and sputtering, sometimes accompanied by pacing and cursing

195

- Shutting down and becoming withdrawn or refusing to engage/talk
- Avoidance (turning attention to something pleasurable like computer or music to avoid work)
- Flight (storming out or leaving the office)

Sometimes the trigger can be auditory, visual, or tactile overstimulation. Whatever the reason, often the best solution is for the student to leave the source of the stress for a while and regroup. Students need to understand how to recognize and manage stress.

Getting Along With Others on the Job

Students with poor social skills should be encouraged to work with a therapist (on or off campus) to improve their pragmatic skills. They might also benefit from joining a support group of others in their relative age group, if available. Also, a mentor or job coach obtained through Vocational Rehabilitation can support the student in developing and improving social skills in addition to focusing on the actual job responsibilities.

Students with particularly weak social skills may need to work on identifying "safe" topics to discuss with others and guidelines to follow when talking with others. In addition to helping students identify nonverbal cues, mentors can assist students with important matters of protocol, such as not referring to people in a derogatory fashion, not correcting people even though they are perceived to have made a mistake, and not leaving a conversation without some kind of closure.

In this chapter we discussed the importance of employment for young people on the autism spectrum. Many of our students come to college with little or no job experience (even babysitting) and require a set of workplace skills to be developed from scratch. On-campus jobs provide great preparation for internships, co-ops, and then off-campus employment. Students must have a supervised opportunity to learn how to be a team player on the job. In this way they will be able to use their skills (academic and work related) to find meaningful employment after college, which is after all central to why we encouraged them to go to school and actively supported their success along the way.

Molly waited until after she graduated from college to begin the process of deciding about jobs versus graduate school, where to live, etc. She worked hard her last semester, received help with her résumé from Career Services, and then enjoyed graduation with her family. After graduating, Molly moved home for a few months and worked with a career counselor to narrow her options about jobs and grad school. Though the transition to living at home was difficult, because Molly had to shift back to living less independently and resume her role as a participating member of the family, Molly and her family decided it was best considering that she needed to pay full attention on college in her last semester and now could use all her time to explore careers (with some help and structure from the career counselor).

Conclusion

Transition to college is one of the top three most difficult transitions a student makes (along with going to kindergarten, finishing college and going to work). Not surprisingly, transition to college is particularly challenging for students on the spectrum. While college can be difficult at first, with appropriate supports and good planning, higher education can be the next step in the educational experiences students need in order to be better prepared for the world of work. Indeed for some, the opportunities college offers to find "like-minded" people was for Stephen Shore (2003), a professor, author, and international consultant who has AS, like finding heaven. Dr. Shore entitled the chapter in his autobiography that discusses his experience in college as "Heaven at Last – in College," going on to state "At college I met people who appreciated me for who I was instead of making fun of what was different about me" (p. 89).

College can take many forms for students. It is essential for clinicians, parents, and high school professionals to remember that there is so much more to higher education than attending classes at a four-year college and living in a residence hall. It is important that we not let our vision of a "typical college experience" blur a student's plans for a good education and a good future.

We hear many parents say, "I want my son/daughter to have what I had in college." Though this feeling is understandable, it may not be appropriate for a given student. The lifestyle of a very social parent is not a reasonable plan for most students on the spectrum.

Nor is a residential college appropriate for a student who needs to develop executive functioning skills, and, therefore, would do better to live at home while attending a community college.

We need to lobby our local and state governments to support the development of technical colleges, trade schools, and community colleges (with residential options) so that our students can gain practical experience and further develop the social and cognitive skills that are hard to develop at home. Often young people are reluctant to accept advice and training from their parents or other care givers, but will learn better when they are actually thrust into a learning situation such as a residence hall or classroom. Students with AS need to experience developing relationships outside the family.

It is essential for clinicians, parents, and high school professionals to remember that there is so much more to higher education than attending classes at a four-year college and living in a residence hall.

We are in an exciting period of time when new programs in four-year colleges and universities are being developed constantly, and new approaches are being tried for students with AS. Such programs did not exist as little as 10 years ago, and very few as recently as five. We have seen an exciting upsurge in programming and service delivery for students on the spectrum. We need to work together – parents, clinicians, educators, employers, college personnel, and researchers – to continue to develop and refine programs for students across the country, across the spectrum. Equally important is developing these programs so our students can develop skills, get an education, and find appropriate work. In today's economy that is a difficult goal. However, with the current statistics of 1 in 110 children being diagnosed with autism (Centers for Disease Control and Prevention, 2011), it is a very necessary goal.

We are in an exciting period of time when new programs in "regular" four-year colleges and universities are being developed constantly, and new approaches are being tried for students with AS.

The numbers of children diagnosed with a spectrum disorder has been increasing, and most of this increase is at the milder edges of the spectrum. It is this group of able students who are and will continue to be a target population of new students with disabilities on campuses nationwide.

College has historically been a starting point for career development in academically talented students. This population has slowly grown to include students with all disabilities. Our newest and (perhaps) most compelling group is the focus of this book – students with AS. If our spectrum students are to participate in the American Dream, we believe that some form of postsecondary education is vital.

Some students will go into vocational training or trade schools. Others will thrive in two-year or certificate colleges. Yet others will be able to successfully transition into four-year college programs, including graduate and professional degree-granting institutions. This book, along with our previous publication (Wolf, Thierfeld Brown, & Bork, 2009), was written to ensure that these academically talented students are supported in college and on to employment.

As parents we know how difficult transitions are. We are each going through major transitions with sons and daughters on the spectrum as we write this conclusion. One is turning 18 and going through probate for guardianship, one is moving to a new high school, and a third is moving to college. We know the difficulty in changing trusted staff and teachers, in trying to give more independence while worrying about everything from hygiene to bullying.

Finally, as a special note to parents – none of us chose to have these incredible children on the autism spectrum, yet we continue to work to improve life for this increasing population. We love and care for our children on the spectrum while helping siblings and family members understand and hopefully accept them. We applaud and thank you for your passion and determination. Together we will work to improve the educational and career options and outcomes.

References

Americans With Disabilities Act. http://www.ada.gov

Buron, K. D. (2007). *A 5 is against the law: Social boundaries straight up! An honest guide for teens and young adults.* Shawnee Mission, KS: AAPC Publishing.

Centers for Disease Control and Prevention (CDC). (2011). *How many children have autism?* Retrieved from http://www.cdc.gov/ncbddd/features/counting-autism.html.

Differences Between IDEA and ADA. www.ccdanet.org/differenceschart.html

Disability Rights and Educational Defense Fund. http://www.dredf.org

Federal Educational Rights and Privacy Act. http://www.ferpa.gov

Individuals With Disabilities Education Act. http://www.idea.ed.gov

Job Behaviors: Why do young adults lose their jobs? http://www.finaid.wwu.edu/studentjobs/students/resources/job_behaviors.php

Manifestation Determination Definition. http://definitions.uselegal.com/m/manifestation-determination

Rehabilitation Act Section 504. http://www.hhs.gov/OCR/504pdf

Shore, S. M. (2003). *Beyond the wall. Personal experiences with autism and Asperger Syndrome* (2nd ed.). Shawnee Mission, KS: AAPC Publishing.

Smart Pens. http://livescribe.com

TRIO Programs. http://www.ed.gov/about/offices/list/ope/trio/index.html

Wolf, L., Thierfeld Brown, J., & Bork, R. (2009). *Students with Asperger Syndrome: A guide for college personnel.* Shawnee Mission, KS: AAPC Publishing.

Wrightslaw. http://www.wrightslaw.com

Recommended Readings

Attwood, T. (1998). *Succeeding in college with Asperger Syndrome.* **London: Jessica Kingsley Publishers.**

Information and practical strategies to help students prepare for studying, interacting with staff and fellow students, coping with expectations and pressure, and understanding their academic and independent responsibilities.

Baker, J. (2005). *Preparing for life: The complete guide to transitioning to adulthood for autism and asperger's syndrome.* **Arlington, TX: Future Horizons.**

User-friendly lesson plans to assist young people in navigating the world post high school.

Bissonette, B. (2010). *Asperger's syndrome workplace survival guide: A neurotypical's secrets for success.* **Stow, NH: Forward Motion Coaching.**

Practical advice for young adults on the spectrum who are making the transition from being a successful student to becoming a successful employee. A major emphasis is on how to get and how to keep a job.

Buron, K. D. (2007). *A 5 is against the law: Social boundaries straight up! An honest guide for teens and young adults.* **Shawnee Mission, KS: AAPC Publishing.**

This book focuses on behaviors that can have serious implications for adolescents and young adults who have difficulty understanding and maintaining social boundaries. Guidance and recommendations for creating scales to manage one's anxiety are provided.

Buron, K., Thierfeld Brown, J., Curtis, M., & King. L. (2012). *Self-management and social behaviors: 5-point scales for adolescents and adults.* **Shawnee Mission, KS: AAPC Publishing.**

Using the concept of 5-point scales, issues of college, work, and adulthood are explored. The authors have developed a different, age-appropriate way of teaching self-management in social situations.

Freedman, S. (2010). *Developing college skills in students with autism and asperger's syndrome.* **London: Jessica Kingsley Publishers.**

The author identifies several skill sets, along with effective intervention strategies for facilitating skill development throughout the student's elementary, middle, and high school years to ensure students on the spectrum are better prepared for their adult lives.

Grandin, T. (1986). *Emergence: Labeled autistic.* **Novato, CA: Warner Books.**

Misunderstood by many, yet supported by a number of important influences, the author has been able to overcome many of her difficulties and gain a Ph.d. as well as become the world's best known adult with autism.

Grandin, T. (1996). *Thinking in pictures: And other reports from my life with autism.* **New York, NY: First Vintage Books Inc.**

This is the second volume of Temple Grandin's personal story.

Grandin, T., & Duffy, K. (2008). *Developing talents: Careers for individuals with Asperger Syndrome and high-functioning autis*m (rev. ed.). **Shawnee Mission, KS: AAPC Publishing.**

An in-depth look at job training and placement for individuals on the spectrum. Possible career paths and matching strengths and skills to vocation are explored.

Hammerschmidt, E. (2008). *Born on the wrong planet.* Shawnee Mission, KS: AAPC Publishing.

A young adult's autobiography highlighting experiences with college, employment, and most recently married life.

Pease, A., & Pease, B. (2006). *The definitive book of body language.* New York, NY: Bantam Books.

This book examines each component of nonverbal communication and body language and gives students the basic vocabulary to read attitudes and emotions through behavior.

Perner, L. (n.d.). *Preparing to be nerdy where nerdy can be cool: College planning for students on the autism spectrum.* Retrieved from http://www.professorsadvice.com.

Results of AS college surveys; describes the kinds of services that some postsecondary institutions may offer to students on the spectrum.

Plank, A. (2011). *Wrong planet.* Retrieved from http://www.wrongplanet.net.

This is a web community designed for individuals (and parents/professionals of those) with autism spectrum and related disorders.

Prince-Hughes, D. (2002). *Aquamarine Blue 5: Personal stories of college students with aspergers.* Athens, GA: Swallow Press.

A compendium of narratives written by college students on the autism spectrum profiling their individual challenges and strengths experienced in the college setting.

Rothenberg, S. (2011). The AS student's guide to the college social scene. *AANE News, 13.* Retrieved from http://www.aane.org/asperger_resources/articles/adults/college_student_asperger.html.

Very detailed recommendations for appropriate and effective behavior in different college social situations.

Segar, M. (1997). *A survival guide for people with Asperger Syndrome*. Retrieved from http://www.autismandcomputing. org.uk/marc2en.html.

In this autobiography, the author explains common everyday situations that can be challenging for individuals with AS but that neurotypicals do not need to learn. "The difficulty with life is that every situation is so different."

Schelvan, R., Smith Myles, B., & Troutman, M. (2004). *The hidden curriculum: Practical solutions for understanding unstated rules in social situations*. **Shawnee Mission, KS: AAPC Publishing.**

A practical approach to helping people on the spectrum understand the hidden rules associated with social interaction.

Shore, S. M. (Ed.). (2004). *Ask and tell: Self-advocacy and disclosure for people on the autistic spectrum*. **Shawnee Mission, KS: AAPC Publishing.**

A collection of voices on the spectrum about the pros and cons of disclosure.

Simone, R. (2010). *Asperger's on the job: Must-have advice for people with asperger's or high functioning autism, and their employers, educators, and advocates*. Arlington, TX: Future Horizons.

Every chapter in this book includes a section called "What the employee can do?" that presents thoughtful and reasonable suggestions. That section is followed by a segment called "To employers and advocates," in which the author counsels the boss of employees with AS to be more tolerant of their differences.

Willey, L. H. (1999). *Pretending to be normal: Living with asperger's syndrome*. **London: Jessica Kingsley Publishers.**

Especially helpful in this book is the list of Survival Skills for College Students in the appendix.

Winner, M. G. (2009). *Socially curious and curiously social: The social thinking guidebook for bright teens and young adults.* **London: Jessica Kingsley Publishers.**

This animé-illustrated guidebook is written for teens and young adults to help them learn how the social mind is expected to work in order to effectively relate to others at school, at work, in the community, and at home.

Wolf, L., Thierfeld Brown, J., & Bork, R. (2009). *Students with Asperger Syndrome: A guide for college personnel.* **Shawnee Mission, KS: AAPC Publishing.**

A guide for staff and faculty at colleges to best practices for working with students on the autism spectrum. This book is also helpful for families looking to understand the world of higher education for students on the spectrum.

Other Related AAPC Books

Developing Talents: Careers for Individuals with Asperger Syndrome and High-Functioning Autism

by Temple Grandin and Kate Duffy; Foreword by Tony Attwood

Code: 9027
Price: $21.95

Becoming Remarkably Able: Walking the Path to Talents, Interests, and Personal Growth

by Jackie Marquette, Ph.D.

Code: 9992
Price: $24.95

Asperger Syndrome: An Owner's Manual 2 For Older Adolescents and Adults: What You, Your Parents and Friends, and Your Employer, Need to Know

by Ellen S. Heller Korin, M.Ed.

Code: 9996
Price: $18.95

About the Authors

Jane Thierfeld Brown, EdD, is director of student services at the University of Connecticut School of Law and co-director of College Autism Spectrum. She has worked in disability services for 33 years. Dr. Brown's main research interests are students with Asperger Syndrome in higher education and students with disabilities in high-stakes graduate programs. She consults with many institutions of higher education, as well as with parents and students on issues of students with autism spectrum disorders, and is a frequent speaker at conferences. She co-authored *Students With Asperger Syndrome: A Guide for College Personnel.* Dr. Brown has three children, the youngest of whom is a 20-year-old son on the spectrum.

Lorraine Wolf, EdD, is the director of disability services at Boston University where she holds faculty appointments as an assistant clinical professor of psychiatry at the School of Medicine and an adjunct associate professor of rehabilitation sciences at the Sargent College of Health and Rehabilitation Sciences. She has over 30 years' experience working with individuals with neurodevelopmental disorders and has taught at both the undergraduate and graduate level. Dr. Wolf consults internationally on university accommodations for students with disabilities and has published and presented extensively on clinical as well as legal issues for students with attention and learning disorders, psychiatric disabilities, and autism spectrum disorders. She is co-author of *Students With Asperger Syndrome: A Guide for College Personnel.* She is the parent of twin boys, one of whom is on the autism spectrum.

Lisa King, MEd, is a co-director of College Autism Spectrum, an educational consulting company that provides training and guidance to colleges regarding best practices for working with students on the autism spectrum, in addition to working directly with students on the spectrum and their families as they transition to, through, and beyond college. Additionally, she serves as an access consultant for St. Catherine University. Under the guidance of colleagues and co-authors, Jane Thierfeld Brown and Lorraine Wolf, Ms. King led a two-year pilot program at the University of Minnesota implementing a new model of service: *Strategic Education for Asperger Students.* She is a wife to Chris and mother of Ian and Bryn.

G. Ruth Kukiela Bork, MEd, is past founder, dean, and director of the Disability Resource Center, Northeastern University in Boston. She serves as an adjunct lecturer on disability for the Physician Assistantship, the Counseling Psychology, the Rehabilitation and Special Education, and the Psychology Programs at Northeastern University. In addition, she has served as director of student services at a private high school where she implemented changes to prepare families and students for transition from high school to college. Ms. Bork's professional involvement in disability affairs and advocacy spans 38 years. She has written and spoken on a variety of disability-related topics ranging from employment of students with disabilities, supporting international students with disabilities, coordinating and providing support services in higher education, and high-school-to-college transition of students with disabilities.